Praise for Amir Ghannad and
THE TRANSFORMATIVE LEADER

"If you want to transform your organization's culture, transform yourself first," says Amir Ghannad in *The Transformative Leader*. This concept cuts to the heart of this insightful, yet very practical book, with numerous take-ways and tools for you to start your transformation now. What's holding you back? Actually, Amir covers that as well. Apply the principles in this impactful book and your life and your organization will transform.

Mike Hoseus
Co-author *Toyota Culture - The Heart and Soul of the Toyota Way*
2009 Shingo Research Award Winner

With a compelling message grounded in connecting examples, Amir unlocks leadership awareness and provides simple and effective approaches to allow any leader at any state in their personal development journey to make real progress in developing their intentional leadership self. *The Transformative Leader* enables you to discover the leader within you as opposed to changing you into one. Armed with insights and understanding you will be equipped to develop and grow your organization's culture of engagement and as a result performance.

Greg Flickinger, Ph.D.
Vice President of Manufacturing and Corporate Engineering at
Snyder-Lance Inc.

Very few leaders were born ready to lead. In most cases, leadership is only mastered after years of trial and error. This book captures the genuine and ever so elusive spirit of great leaders. It takes the essence of what would otherwise take years to learn and breaks it down into powerful, tangible, attainable behaviors that can be achieved by anyone strong enough to live by them. This book takes organizational wisdom and turns it into teachable practices. The Transformative Leader should be read and re-read by any manager who wishes to make a difference!

Reut Schwartz-Hebron
Senior Consultant
Founder of the Key Change Institute
Author of *Making Difficult Change Simple*

Amir Ghannad has drawn on his wealth of personal and professional experiences to write a practical and powerful book on what it takes to be an effective leader and to change the culture around you. *The Transformative Leader* is an easy read and filled with lessons anyone in a position of responsibility for leading others can put to immediate good use. His twenty 'One Point Lessons'—each no more than a few pages and each making a solid point—are especially powerful. Each makes an important point on its own, and collectively they encompass what it takes to be a great leader.

Bill Waddell
Consultant and Principal at Bill Waddell Manufacturing
Leadership Support
Co-author of *Rebirth of American Industry, Evolving Excellence,* and
Simple Excellence

Amir does an amazing job of providing both conceptual and practical approaches to transforming a culture from within. *The Transformative Leader* is a must read for anyone who wants to see the vision and values of their company consistently displayed across the entire organization.

Nathan Artt
Owner/President at Ministry Solutions

THE
TRANSFORMATIVE
LEADER

THE
TRANSFORMATIVE
LEADER

Boldly Declare,
Courageously Pursue,
and Abundantly Achieve
the Extraordinary

AMIR GHANNAD

THE
GHANNAD
GROUP, LLC

THE
GHANNAD
GROUP, LLC

The Ghannad Group, LLC
Atlanta, Georgia

10 9 8 7 6 5 4 3 2   0 1 2 5 1 4
| | | |

Cover design by Naseem Ghannad
Cover and Interior Arrow Icon made by Sergiu Bagrin from
www.flaticon.com, licensed under Creative Commons
Interior Compass Icon made by Freepik from www.flaticon.com
Editing by Naseem Ghannad
Proofreading & Copyediting by Naveed Ghannad
Author photograph by Naseem Ghannad

ISBN: 978-0-9967741-0-9

Printed in the United States of America

This paper meets the requirements of ANSI/NISO Z39.48-1992

DEDICATION

This book is dedicated to my soulmate and wife of over 33 years, Connie, whose wisdom, abundant love, and unfailing encouragement have made everything I love about my life possible.

I am forever grateful to my parents, Habibollah Ghannad and Mehrangiz Partovi Deilami, for laying the foundation for who I am during the first 16 years of my life, and for having the courage to sacrifice so much to send me off to the U.S. from Iran as a young boy, just so I would have a chance at a better life.

I'd like to thank my son, Naveed, and my daughter, Naseem, for being two of my greatest teachers and coaches. Striving to be more like them keeps me growing. Without their guidance and suggestions, this book might have never come to fruition.

I'd like to acknowledge my brothers, Dr. Mohammad Ali Ghannad and Dr. Afshin Ghannad, and their families, for their unconditional love for me and my family, which has always been abundantly expressed on our visits to Iran, and in between visits from afar.

I would also like to thank my "brothers from other mothers," my group of friends in Atlanta known as the PPA, who have been closer to me than most brothers are to one another, and whose friendship and brotherly love for the past 36 years has been something that most people yearn for, but only a few are fortunate enough to experience. Most especially, I am grateful to my dearest friend, the late Hamid Daftarian, whose vision of who I was and what I had to offer was always bigger than my own. I know he is smiling in Heaven for my finally having published my first book.

I'd like to acknowledge all the people who had to put up with me trying to lead them when I had no idea what I was doing, especially during the early years of my career at Procter and Gamble. I learned many of the lessons in this book inadvertently at their expense and they deserve much credit for anything positive I have accomplished as a leader.

Most importantly, I am grateful for the grace of God, which has carried me through challenges under which I would have been crushed had I relied only on my own strength.

Amir Ghannad

"Only from the heart can you touch the sky."
                                          - Rumi

CONTENTS

FOREWORD

When Amir asked me to write the foreword to his book, *The Transformative Leader*, two things led me to jump at the opportunity. The first was Amir himself. We met at the 2015 Shingo Institute Annual Conference, and while we were both speaking at the event, my responsibilities as Senior Curriculum Advisor and member of the Shingo Executive Committee kept me from sitting in on his session. The impact of his message, however, was felt immediately. Client after client came up to me and said, "Did you sit in on the session by Amir Ghannad? He was great, and his approach is totally aligned with [that of your book,] *Own the Gap*."

Later during the event, I had a chance to better understand their excitement. Amir stopped by our booth and introduced himself. What stuck with me immediately was his warmth, humility, and genuine passion for people and the principles of operational excellence. It was easy to see why my clients were so engaged with both Amir and his message.

The second reason that I agreed to write this foreword was that, when Amir explained the focus of his book, he referenced a section on leadership out of *Own the Gap*; the reference was to the three essential characteristics of trust, tenacity, and humility, that each leader needs in order to be successful in causing a culture transformation. Ultimately, a leader's ability to embrace the role of a learner (humility) and have the commitment to follow through in the face of adversity (tenacity) become the primary drivers of building trust. As trust is the key ingredient of engagement, these characteristics—what I call T2H—form a powerful and interconnected framework from which to both grow leaders, as well as evaluate future leaders.

While developing T2H leaders is critical for success, the focus of *Own the Gap* is the development of daily management systems, not leaders. So when Amir connected the essence of Transformative Leadership to a topic which was not done justice in my own book, I was hooked. My hope was to discover a book that unapologetically puts the importance of what's on the inside of each leader to the forefront and gave these characteristics the attention they deserved. *The Transformative Leader* is just that book.

The Transformative Leader makes it clear from the start that successful cultural transformation depends on leadership, and proper leadership depends upon our willingness to own our gaps and seek to first transform ourselves before we transform the organization. A leader's goal, then, is to first inspire themselves to appreciate the power of a culture where teams can—and will— own their business outcomes and improve performance each and every day. To accomplish this, it is critical for leaders to own their unique role in the transformation. When a *kaizen* culture is your objective, leaders are called to become servants of those whom they lead, while at the same time recognizing that how a leader "shows up" directly correlates to a team's willingness and ability to own their outcomes. In this way, *The Transformative Leader* sets aside the notion that leadership is primarily an exercise in "what you do," and rather demonstrates that being a great leader is first and foremost about "who you are."

What makes *The Transformative Leader* a powerful read, is the challenge it issues to each and every one of us tasked with inspiring and leading others toward the consistent achievement of organizational outcomes. Anyone who has been placed in a position to influence and support others is a leader. In that respect, Amir's words can equally apply to any member of a team whose goal is to contribute to the development of a culture of continuous improvement where "improving the work, is the work." Therein lies the power of his message, and it is a message that I believe will help innumerable organizations in their quest to create a principle-based culture of continuous improvement.

As I enter into my third decade of helping organizations improve performance and transform their cultures, I would like to believe that my work embodies the leadership spirit that Amir challenges each of us to recognize and own in *The Transformative Leader*. It is this spirit of making the decision to be "The One" to make a difference, owning our leadership gaps, having clarity of intent, and embracing humility in our interactions with others which seems to me to be at the core of our success as change agents.

Michael Martyn
Founder, SISU Consulting Group
Co-Author of *Own the Gap*
2012 Shingo Research Award Winner

INTRODUCTION

Imagine a world where the workplace is a source of inspiration rather than a source of anguish and frustration. It's a place where employees experience growth and development, and where they bring their best to work every single day. They are loyal to their employer and know that their employer cares about them as people, not just as interchangeable tools that serve particular functions; they collaborate with, and generously contribute to one another and experience an abundance of satisfaction. The team is out to win and they use guidelines and standards as a solid foundation to build on, not a ceiling that inhibits their creativity and autonomy. The objectives of the employees and the employer are inseparable, so people don't have to choose between doing what is right for the company and what is good for them personally. They—employees and company—not only deliver superior results but have an inherent desire to get better that keeps them moving forward.

If all of this sounds a bit too "Pollyanna," or if it sparks some cynicism in your mind, it is because the great majority of us have given up on creating such environments in our workplaces and have settled for something far less satisfying or profitable. We all want to be part of a team like that, but we often get overwhelmed at the thought of what it would take to create such a culture. We see it as the responsibility of someone else with more power than us to transform our workplace. Even those of us who take on making it happen often don't know where to start, and consequently, we quickly become overwhelmed and give up. Even if we somehow managed to overcome this personal roadblock, we may have eventually given up in the face of the organizational force to maintain the status quo.

But what if it really could be done? What would be the benefit to the individuals and the business unit? What if we figured out a way to deliver benchmark results and have the people in our organization fired up about constantly getting better? What would happen to the profitability and productivity of the team, business unit, or the company for that matter? What kind of prosperity and peace of mind would it create in the lives of the people in that workplace, their families, and acquaintances? What kind of far-reaching impact would the cultivation of such workplace culture have on the economy and the well-being of a nation, and, I dare say, the world?

I'd like you to set aside all your objections and questions for a moment and just dwell on the personal impact it would have on your life to be part of the kind of team that I have described here. Think about what it would do for you mentally, physically, financially, and emotionally to be part of a grand experiment such as the creation of this kind of workplace. Now, think about what it would take to create such a workplace environment.

Where would you start? What button would you push and what lever would you pull? Who is responsible for making it happen? What would be the process of changing the culture and results from what they are today to what you would want them to be? What would you do differently? What would your boss do differently? Is it even possible to deliver superior results and empower and engage the organization at the same time? How would you find time to do what needs to be done to change the culture and environment of your workplace in the face of multiple priorities and the rapid pace of change? Can you do anything about it in your position or will someone much higher than you on the organizational chart need to make it happen? Is it worth the trouble to even try for this? What is your boss going to think of you if you question some of the practices that go against the current norms of your present workplace? What about your peers? Will they join you or talk about you behind your back? What other barriers could get in the way and how will you overcome them?

You may be part of an organization that is already operating at peak performance and nurturing the team for a better future. If that is the case, you are extremely fortunate. You are also a member of a rare group, because most people are grappling with many perceived or real barriers to progress that have caused them to resign themselves to the status quo, futilely hoping that something will change someday.

I don't mean to preach a message of gloom and doom, but I think you would agree that most of our workplaces fall far short of the kind of workplace culture I described earlier. Our results tend not to be extraordinary and our people are not engaged or enthusiastic about their work. According to Gallop's *2013 State of the American Workforce Report*, only 30% of employees are engaged, 52% are not engaged, and 18% are actively disengaged. The *AON Hewitt 2014 Trends in Global Employee Engagement* report says that globally, only 22% of employees are highly engaged, and 16% are actively disengaged. Acknowledging that this problem exists and that it could be detrimental to our success is the first step in altering the inevitable, default future and replacing it with the designed future that we are out to create.

The good news is that solving this problem is much simpler than one might think. Sure, every person and workplace is different and the specific actions must be tailored to each unique situation, but it all comes down to one thing, and that's *leadership*. Without effective leadership, the culture and results of an organization will invariably stay the same or get worse, no matter how much people within the organization want change. We all know that intuitively, but what exactly does leadership look like and whose responsibility is it? Countless books have been written that explain the various components and key factors of effective leadership. So, why this book? What makes this book different?

The answer is simple. This book is about compelling and enabling you to rediscover the Transformative Leader within yourself. It is about acting on what you inherently know to be effective rather than forcing yourself to follow contrived, rigid procedures with inconsistent or unsustainable results. Although you may learn something new about leadership through your reading, the main purpose of this book is not to teach you something or tell you what to do. My purpose in writing this book is to facilitate the process of you gaining the wisdom that you need about your specific situation, and of you relating to yourself as the Transformative Leader that you already are.

While I believe in certain timeless and universal principles of leadership, I do not believe in cookie-cutter leadership development. My approach is to introduce ideas and concepts, which will trigger in you the desire to explore and discover what is in the way of you showing up as the leader that you are right now.

I am certain you already have beliefs about leadership that have been reinforced to you over and over again through your experiences throughout your life and career. These beliefs have gotten you to where you are, and while many of them are empowering beliefs that have produced much success for you in the past, many of them are also limiting and disempowering beliefs that keep you from even greater success in the future.

Perhaps you are happy with where you are, or perhaps you are looking for a way out of your current circumstances. Regardless of which camp you belong to, my job is to compel you to reach beyond good *and* great, and go for the extraordinary!

I am committed to you experiencing paradigm-altering "ah-ha!" moments that will shift your view of who you are as a leader, and what you are capable of accomplishing right at this very moment. My promise is that the benefits of these lessons will go beyond just delivering results at your workplace, and go on to amplify the impact you have on the lives of those who count on you for leadership, the lives of their families, and the world at large.

I believe Transformative Leadership is the key component that will distinguish the truly extraordinary companies from the merely good and great ones in the coming decade. The rapid rate of technological advances over the past few decades has accelerated the pace and magnitude of improvements to work processes and results of organizations. We have explored and applied methodologies aimed at solving problems with the quality of our products and services, with levels of waste in our processes, with the efficiency of our business practices, and with the impact we are having on the planet. We have found ways to seek and use the relevant information in and about our businesses on a real time basis. We have automated our work processes to reduce our reliance on labor. These advances are being made at speeds that were unimaginable just a few years ago and no doubt, the tools, systems, and methodologies that are available to us in just a few short years will be far more sophisticated than they are today. However, the key facet that we have yet to scratch the surface of is the power of Transformative Leadership to harness the human potential of everyone within the workforce, both individually and, to exponentially greater effect, collectively.

Companies that provide fair pay and benefits, and don't take their people for granted have always done better than others, but maintaining these practices is no longer a competitive advantage simply because they have become industry standards that are now regarded as common sense. How this came about can be attributed to a variety of causes, be it because companies were forced by laws that were established to protect employees from employers, or because of the fear of employees organizing against the company, or because of the genuine desire to treat employees right. Regardless of how the industry came to this place, the fact is that these ideas and practices do not hold the power they once did to make a company great. Today, the main competitive advantage is to go far beyond what is merely *required* and to create an environment in which the employees *choose* to go beyond the call of duty and become the cause for the company to flourish and evolve organically.

I have mentioned that the focus of this book is to cause you to experience the full benefit of being the Transformative Leader that is within you already. Ultimately, however, your journey cannot be about you for it to be fruitful. It must be focused on you causing a transformation in others in your organization and creating an explosion of empowerment and extraordinary results as a consequence. It is all about unleashing the potential of the people around you who, by the way, are the ones operating all the expensive machinery, interfacing with your customers, administering the state of the art work processes, and executing the systems in which you have made significant investment.

Although we don't know each other personally, I do know that you and I are kindred spirits in that we share an interest in improving our effectiveness as leaders, both in our workplaces and life in general. My intention in writing this book is to support you in your journey by introducing you to paradigms, approaches, and tools that go above and beyond traditional leadership teachings that have been around for years. I am committed to you not only finding new, practical tools that you can put to work immediately, but also experiencing a shift in how you relate to yourself as a leader, and discovering hidden keys that will unleash your potential and supercharge your ability to transform any environment in which you choose to declare yourself a leader, no matter where you are on the organizational chart.

To those of you wondering whether this book is for you, let me assure you that it is, and let me explain how I am so certain. Most ineffective leaders who try to beat people into submission have no interest in learning more about leadership. Therefore, I know that you are either a good leader or a great one already, and that you are also looking to get better. No matter where you see yourself on this spectrum, my promise to you is that if you read this book with the intention to take your leadership effectiveness to the next level, you will find what you are looking for. I also promise to not just stop at introducing ideas, but to assist you in developing a deeper understanding of them and to guide you through practical steps to apply them to your specific situation. The other good news about this book is that what is contained within it is entirely independent of your level of experience. Whether you are new to leadership or have years of experience in leading organizations, and whether you are the leader of a team of two or an organization of thousands, my promise to you is that you will be able to apply what is presented here in the context of exactly where you are now, and where you intend to take yourself and your organization in the future.

I hope that the contents of this book will be a blessing to you, your family, the people in your organization, and their families as well.

HOW TO GET THE MOST OUT OF THIS BOOK

In order for you to get the most out of this book, I'd like to tell you a little about how it's organized so you know what to expect, and make a few suggestions for you to consider during your reading. The first of those suggestions being that I highly recommend that you not skip this section.

To begin, let me address how the book is laid out. In the spirit of beginning with the end in mind, we will first examine the characteristics of a high performance culture. While it is often easy to articulate the desirable results and specific targets that the team or organization is after, the tricky part is defining the characteristics of the culture that will reliably deliver and sustain those results. I will place a great deal of emphasis on these characteristics with the intent to cause you to wrap your mind around the specific transformation you are out to create.

We will then look at the mindset, necessary attitude, and foundational approaches that are conducive to *being* a Transformative Leader before we discuss *doing* the things that leaders do. This section will help you to examine your mindset as a leader and identify the beliefs and approaches that are working for you, and the ones that you would like to modify.

Next, we will highlight various aspects of what it takes to show up as a Transformative Leader in a series of One Point Lessons (OPLs). You're welcome to cover the OPLs in any order that best suits you. Although, going over them as they are laid out

THE TRANSFORMATIVE LEADER

is the simplest approach, you may choose to thumb through them, take a look at the section called "The Bottom Line," and first read and apply the ones that are most applicable to you.

Each OPL includes reflection questions and recommended follow-up actions to help you solidify your takeaways and guide you in planning how to put them to good use. Additionally, I have provided a set of tools and forms in the appendix which will support you in the practical application of what you read. I have created a free printable workbook with all of the one point lesson and appendix questions with space for you to write your answers. For access to the free workbook, type this url into your browser: www.amirghannad.com/ttlworkbook

Now that you know more about the flow of the book, let me go over a few points that I believe will prepare you to get the most out of the book.

While reading, you may find yourself experiencing two types of learning. The first is *informative learning*, which involves you being armed with knowledge you did not have before. This type of learning is, indeed, very valuable and necessary in order to develop competence in any field, including leadership effectiveness. The second is *transformative learning*, which has to do with gaining insight about your own situation and discovering what is currently in the way, so you can get it out of the way.

It is important to recognize that although this book does contain coaching on several practical tools, approaches, and their effective use, the final ingredient that will cause you to have a transformative experience is your willingness to examine how the concepts apply to your personal experience at this point in your journey. The insight and wisdom that is revealed to you relative to your specific situation is always far more beneficial than any theoretical knowledge you can gain from an external source.

This type of learning is an inside-out process and it often

brings about a whole new paradigm that completely shifts how you relate to yourself and the world around you. I experienced this a few years ago in an assignment that involved a major turnaround in results. Relying on what I knew, I started taking steps that I felt needed to be taken and we began to make some progress. However, we soon hit a plateau and found ourselves stuck, until I discovered things that *I didn't know that I didn't know*. I am referring to things like the *realization* that the greatest barrier to progress was my own self-righteousness and refusal to embrace a style that was different than the one that had always worked for me in the past. Once this was revealed to me and I went to work on it, we went on to make extraordinary progress. In less than two years, we were delivering the best results in the company and surpassing industry benchmarks in several areas. As a bonus, we also enjoyed all the benefits of sky-rocketing morale that no one had thought possible just a couple of years earlier.

Having an epiphany can completely transform your world view and experience of life, and most of the time it comes out of nowhere, when you least expect it. In my case, I remember the exact day, like it was yesterday, when it became clear to me that the problem was not something *out there*, but rather in how I related to the challenges I was facing. I also remember that just prior to that, I had been busy doing more of what hadn't been working, and simply playing "whack-a-mole" with my issues. My intention throughout this book, is to create a transformative experience for you that allows you to have many of these same types of realizations.

Unfortunately, leaving yourself open to that type of revelation is not a straightforward process. It is not about following a *linear* path of learning one thing and then another, rather it's quite the opposite. It requires *lateral* thinking, that you go against your natural tendency to build on what you already know, and instead, explore counterintuitive approaches that are discontinuous and could yield major breakthroughs. This section of the book serves to prepare you to not simply learn what is being taught, but to, more importantly, make you aware of why you are not acting on what you already know. It requires you to truly leave yourself open to receiving new insights. In other words, you must discover what is in the way and get it out of the way, so that you can move forward at a rate that you hadn't thought possible.

As the saying goes, "when the student is ready, the teacher will appear." You will get what you are ready to receive and that is just fine, but to enhance your experience, I'd ask you to consider the following:

Did you hear what I said? – Beware of the secretary of your brain, also known as your Reticular Activating System (RAS). It is perfectly designed and programmed to give you access to what you already believe, filter in the information you are interested in, and filter everything else out. This part of our mental anatomy serves a very important function, in that it keeps us sane by not letting our brains get overloaded with useless information. The downside, however, is that it also blocks out some pertinent information.

You may not be conscious of how your RAS works, but you definitely experience its impact on a daily basis. Have you ever bought a new car and then started seeing the same kind of car everywhere? Have you ever been in a crowded room, concentrating on the conversation you were having with one person, blocking out all of the other noise, and then suddenly heard your name mentioned across the room? That is your RAS hard at work to make sure you are not bothered by stuff that you are not interested in, and filtering in what might be of interest to you.

One of the most fascinating (and perhaps funny) ways I have experienced this since moving to the US in 1978 with a very limited English vocabulary, was when native English speakers would consistently hold off on using words that I didn't know until I learned them (or so I thought). As soon as I learn a new word, suddenly it's on TV, in conversations, in books, everywhere, after never hearing or seeing the word in over 30 years! Of course, the word was being uttered around me for years, but I just ignored it because I had no idea what it meant.

So, it is perfectly natural that you will miss many key concepts in this book, simply because you are not ready to receive them. However, I believe you can increase your chances of getting some valuable insight by just being aware of this phenomenon and keeping an open mind. I do believe that you find what you look for and you see what you look at.

You won't believe a word that I will say to you – I am quite certain of this! As you read this book, even when your RAS allows something to get through, I am sure you won't believe a word. This is because you never believe anything anybody says to you; you only believe what you say to yourself *about* what you hear. A few seconds ago, you might have been saying to yourself, "What is he talking about? Of course, I believe some of the things I hear!" And now, you might be saying to yourself, "Hmmm, I get it." The source of this conversation is that little voice in the back of your mind that sounds just like you, and is constantly reporting what is going on around you. Listening to this internal dialogue is like listening to a baseball game announcer on the radio. You can't see the game, but you can follow what is going on by listening to the announcer's report and seeing the real game in your mind's eye. In the same way, your internal dialogue is going on all the time and interpreting what is going on right in front of you. Your view of what is going on is influenced far more by what you say to yourself about the situation than what you actually physically see or hear.

As you read this book, what you say to yourself will determine what you choose to do with your takeaways. So, pay attention to what you are saying to yourself, and take responsibility for adjusting that internal dialogue to produce the kind of results you want.

It's now or never. Act now! – As you come across various topics in this book, you might say to yourself, "This is interesting, and here is exactly what I am going to do with it." You might also say, "This is hogwash, and it doesn't apply to me." Whatever you do, watch out for the conversation that goes like this: "This is interesting. I should do something with this someday!" Odds are that you won't.

Think of all the things you have been saying you are going to do someday. I don't know about you, but my list is so long, that if "someday" ever gets here, it had better be six months long! There is a restaurant in Atlanta called Joe's Crab Shack®, and on the wall just outside the restaurant, there is a sign that reads: "Free Crab Tomorrow!" As you might have guessed, they haven't served a free crab yet, because it is never tomorrow, it is always only today.

So watch out for your internal dialogue, and be intentional about the decisions you make about what you are going to do with what you get, and by when. Take what you get out of your reading for a test drive immediately by applying it in your life. Don't wait until you have a perfect understanding, or until you are sure it will work. Try it out first and perfect it later. As Jerry Sternin, the author of *The Power of Positive Deviance* put it, "It's easier to act your way into a new way of thinking, than think your way into a new way of acting." Get some wins under your belt and you will be encouraged to stay in action.

What are you committed to? – The best way to personalize your transformative learning process is to think of a specific result you are committed to improving, or a certain outcome you are committed to achieving. Let that be your focus as you read this book and complete the exercises. This causes you to channel what you learn toward something tangible and specific. If I were to give you 10 minutes of internet access to research the solution to a problem, wouldn't you want to know the problem before you started researching? Would it work if you were to aimlessly gather knowledge for 10 minutes, only to find out that only a fraction of what you learned was applicable to the specific problem you were supposed to solve? The same is true here. Pick a cause you are passionate about, and be intentional about learning and discovering what is most helpful to you in your specific journey.

Declare yourself the barrier – I realize that there are many barriers in the way of your progress. You might not have the support of your boss, you may not have adequate staffing or funding, or the culture may not be conducive to you implementing big changes. All of these external circumstances can be very real barriers, but for the purpose of getting the most out of this book, I'd like you to declare yourself the greatest barrier to your progress. Consider that you have either created those other problems, or contributed to them, or at the very least, you have been tolerating them. Look inward, be straight with yourself on your contribution to the problem, and look for solutions. By no means am I suggesting that those external barriers are not the issue. I realize they are real and if they were easy to remove, you would have done it by now. This is precisely why it is important for you to consider yourself the greatest barrier and leave yourself open to understanding why you have not been effective at overcoming those other issues.

Be coachable – One thing all Olympic athletes have in common is that they all have a coach! That's not because they are lousy at what they do, it's because they are great at what they do, and they realize to be even better, they need a coach who can give them objective feedback, encouragement, and motivation to move even further in the right direction. I'd like you to consider me your coach, and to be coachable. This doesn't mean you blindly accept everything I tell you, it just means you are willing to try an idea on for fit before you reject it.

Stay focused – Stay focused on the message in the section you are reading instead of wishing that you would get to the more exciting parts or specific instructions. Some of the most important revelations you will get will come from unlikely places, and you will miss them if you are not present.

I will talk about you – I will make statements about what you do and how you think. Obviously, I realize that I don't know who is going to be reading this book, and that I don't know you personally. I don't claim the statements I make about you to be the truth, but I'd like you to consider them and see if they fit. If they don't, please don't get offended and hold them against me. Toss them to the side and move on to the next point.

It is going to get spicy – I believe in *Spicy Coaching*. I started using this term a couple of years ago when I gave people the choice of "mild" or "spicy" coaching. Mild coaching is no longer on the menu, so spicy, straight coaching is what you'll get. It may sting a little when it is delivered, but it makes a difference. I'd like permission to invade your space a little and be straight about some things that you need to consider. Once again, if it doesn't fit, toss it and let's move on.

Help yourself first, then help others – As much as you might think some of this stuff would be good for someone you know, like your boss or one of your colleagues, use it for yourself first. You will be much more effective in causing a transformation in someone else once you experience one yourself.

Take notes about what is revealed to you – I recommend that you take time to reflect on what you read and separate your notes into at least these three categories:

1. Concepts you learn about

2. Things you discover about yourself and your tendencies that you didn't see previously

3. Actions you are committed to taking and the date by which you will complete them

(I have provided three pages in the notes section at the end of the book for this purpose).

Do the exercises – Be open to trying out the ideas that are presented and do the recommended exercises, whether you feel like it or not. If you hold a glass of water in your hand and turn it upside down, whether you feel like it or not, the water will spill. Likewise, the reflection questions and recommended actions in certain sections of this book are designed to produce certain results and they will do just that, whether you feel like doing them or not.

Share, Share, Share – Discuss what is being revealed to you with others. Share your experience, contribute to them, and let them contribute to you. It is in sharing that we give life to the possibilities we envision in our future.

THE CULTURE
THE TRANSFORMATIVE LEADER CREATES

Before we delve into the attitudes and behaviors of Transformative Leaders, and discuss tools and methodologies with which to cultivate them, it is important that we create the right context for what you are after in the first place. What outcome do you want to create in your team, in your organization, or out in the world? Have you set your sights on a future state that you are excited about, or have you already diminished your vision because you can't imagine things being that great?

I often ask leaders—in many cases, top executives at my seminars—to think of one thing that they are out to transform in their organization. In most cases, I see people looking up at the ceiling, trying to figure out what that thing is. They are all working on a number of important initiatives, but that is not the same as being clear on the ultimate outcome they are out to create. When I have this conversation with leaders in small groups or one-on-one, the tendency is to begin to talk about the problems they are facing in their organization that they would like to solve, or at best, the Key Performance Indicators (KPIs) they are on the hook to deliver. However, there is much more to Transformative Leadership than solving the immediate problems and trying to deliver this quarter's results.

My personal experience is that, while setting clear goals and targets is essential, sometimes it is not enough to keep me in action. In other words, mere numbers on a spreadsheet don't carry the day. It is the emotional connection to what it would be like to have achieved those results that will cause me to hang in there when the going gets tough.

We all want to be part of something significant. Therefore, it is important to express and experience what we are working toward in terms that we deem significant and worthwhile. This is best accomplished by starting with the immediate activities we are engaged in, or with the results we are hoping to achieve in our daily routine. The deeper connection to something meaningful can then be established by asking ourselves "so what?" a few times. Just as asking "why?" a few times helps you uncover the root cause of an issue, asking "so what?" gets you to tie whatever you are doing to the greater purpose it serves in the world. I am reminded of the story of the two brick layers who were asked what they were doing: one responded, "I am laying bricks" and the other said, "I am building a cathedral." Which of these two do you think will have the inclination to go above the call of duty to ensure the job is done well? Of course, it will be the one who can establish the connection between what he is doing and a higher purpose.

Several years ago, I accepted a position as the plant manager of a plant that had historically produced decent results. The plant had recently been acquired by a private equity firm, which was investing in the business and increasing volume and complexity with a lot fewer resources than they had had in the past. In a matter of a couple of months, the house of cards crumbled and we found ourselves being the worst performing plant in the entire company. The only thing worse than our results was our morale!

My team and I had very specific targets that we needed to hit, and I can tell you that the work that had to be done to deliver those numbers would not have gotten done if we hadn't taken the time to tie it to a higher purpose than simply delivering the results. I was very clear—and was frequently reminded by my bosses, in case I had forgotten—that I was responsible for delivering the numbers; but because our morale was so low, and for good reason, I could not see any way to deliver the results without paying significant attention to changing the culture. The higher purpose that I established for myself was to ensure that the people who worked at the plant took pride in their work and didn't go home and "kick the dog" because they were frustrated and burned out. That became the compelling reason that kept me going.

We established a two-part vision, and went on to wrap our minds around what each part meant and what success would look and feel like. The first part of our vision was that we were going to be "The Showcase of Excellence," which meant we would deliver benchmark results in all the predefined performance measures, as well as other standards, that we set for ourselves. The other part of our vision was that we would become "The Cradle of Prosperity," which spoke to the condition of our culture and meant that our workplace would be a source of inspiration to all employees. We wanted to create an experience for everyone such that they would want to go beyond compliance and truly commit to doing what needed to be done in order for our team to succeed.

In the face of seemingly insurmountable challenges, we pressed forward because we were hooked, not just by our targets for efficiency, waste, and other KPIs, but by what it would be like to be working in a place that was delivering those kinds of results. We knew we had to deliver the results, but we began to get excited about the journey and the culture we were creating. In fact, I am certain that if the future we anticipated was one of great results delivered through a culture of dictatorship, muscling, silos, and back-stabbing, we would not have been able to muster up the energy it took to go on to become the best in the company and deliver industry benchmark results in many of our KPIs. We were clear *why* it had to be done and that reason was big enough to keep us in action, even when we were not exactly clear on *what* to do, or *how* to do it.

I firmly believe that what is missing in many organizations today is the emotional connection to the vision for the future. I have yet to come across any individual or organization that has declared that their goal is to be

> *"Everybody wants to be a High Performance Organization, but not many are committed to becoming one."*

mediocre and deliver sub-standard results. Just about every organization out there would like to deliver superior performance. Everyone sets targets, and develops and communicates strategic plans to deliver them. The point is that everybody wants to *be* a High Performance Organization (HPO), but not many are committed to *becoming* one. The mere declaration that you want to be an organization that delivers superior results does not distinguish you from your peers and competitors; actively demonstrating your commitment to the process of becoming one does.

Being an HPO is all about delivering, sustaining, and improving the results that are important to the organization. However, the process of becoming an HPO requires leaders to have a much deeper understanding of how those results are delivered, and of what it takes to bring about a significant and sustainable shift in the culture that engenders the behaviors necessary to produce those results. Becoming an HPO depends largely on creating a culture in which everyone is engaged and committed. This is the type of culture that I will call a High Commitment Culture (HCC).

In essence, we could say that performance is a direct outcome of the culture of an organization, which we could consider to be the sum total of the behaviors that take place in the organization. Hence, the process of transforming an organization into an HPO comes down to creating the desired culture, and therefore requires a certain level of mastery in culture transformation. That is, how to understand and assess various aspects of it, how to leverage it to inspire people, how to influence it, and how to use real-time signals from it to know what course corrections to make.

I believe some leaders are naturally more endowed with the ability to sense the culture and read the subtle signs and naturally influence it, while others have to work harder at it. No matter where you consider yourself to be on this spectrum, the mere recognition that culture—and mastery of it—is a key element of Transformative Leadership sets you apart from those who are oblivious to this important fact and are operating like a bull in a china shop.

"Becoming an HPO depends largely on creating a culture in which everyone is engaged and committed."

I have often found myself in the middle of cultural transformations throughout my career and have learned enough—through the school of hard knocks—to know that there is no finish line when it comes to mastering the art and science of leveraging culture. I have also come to realize that it can be a lot of fun and extremely satisfying to lead an organization through a transition from a culture that is exhausting and doesn't produce the desired results, to one that is exhilarating, energizing, and rewarding for all stakeholders, especially team members.

So, what does an HCC look and feel like? I would define an HCC as one that would encompass and perpetuate the behaviors that best accomplish the team's mission. It certainly looks different for different organizations, but in the end it results in a high level of engagement and commitment. The specifics of the desired culture for each organization are best defined by team members who are passionate about the mission and vision of the team. Having said that, I do believe that there are several cultural characteristics that are universal, though they may be expressed and experienced differently in different parts of the world, or at different locations in a company. For instance, no one would say that keeping people in the dark would bring out the best in them, even though the actual form of engagement and method of giving and receiving input is vastly different in various cultures around the world.

> *"Performance is a direct outcome of the culture of an organization."*

Over the years, as I've taken leadership teams through the process of defining the ideal culture for their organization, what I have found to be effective is to introduce them to several distinctions between an HCC and a traditional culture. This generates a great deal of dialogue within the team and guides them in the process of picking the characteristics that resonate with them, so they can be included in their vision of the ideal culture and their road map to get there.

As you go over these characteristics that distinguish an HCC from a traditional workplace listed on the next few pages, I'd like you to examine where your current culture is relative to each of the characteristics. Ideally, you will notice that your current culture is healthy in some respects. You may also notice that there are certain aspects of your culture that are hindering your progress. Again, the key is to identify a few aspects of the culture that resonate with you and set out to create the specific transformation that your organization would get the most benefit from.

We will address many of these cultural attributes in greater detail later in this book and you will be introduced to plenty of ideas on how to go about transforming certain aspects of your culture. For now, take a glance at the following list with the intent to assess your current culture.

TRADITIONAL	HCC
There is a rule for everything. It is easy to manage by these rules, but it is not very effective.	Principles are established and they guide most of the decisions. Sometimes it is not easy, but it is more effective and productive.
Rewards are based on job titles and/or seniority.	Rewards are based on skill and contribution.
Hard and fast boundaries around jobs; people have limited skills.	Team members are multi-skilled and flow to the work as needed.
Less desirable work is pushed down to more junior roles.	Everyone shares in handling the less desirable work.
Top-down decision making	Shared leadership and decision making
Conservative goals are set based on past limitations.	Stretching goals are inspired by future possibilities.
Division into "Haves" and "Have nots"	Valued and engaged team members at all levels

TRADITIONAL	HCC
Responsibility is given but authority is withheld, or authority is requested without taking responsibility.	Balance of responsibility for results and authority to make or influence decisions that impact them
Low trust	High trust
Compliance focused	Commitment focused
Employees often have to choose between doing what's right for them and what's right for the company.	The interests of the employees and the company are inseparable. There are common objectives that benefit the company and the individuals.
Dictatorship	Servant Leadership
Bosses blame team members for lack of results.	Leaders hold themselves 100% accountable for the results of the team.
Bosses expect everyone to communicate in their language and style.	Leaders adapt their style to people and circumstances.
People work independently in their business units or functional silos, and answer to the boss.	People collaborate across organizational boundaries at all levels to plan the work and deliver results.
Focused on survival	Focused on extraordinary results
Focused on addressing symptoms of problems	Focused on creating the desired future
Entitlement mentality: • Employees feel they are entitled to more compensation. • Bosses feel they are entitled to the employees' full commitment.	Personal accountability: • Employees feel accountable for giving 100%. • Leaders feel accountable for creating an environment where employees offer up their full commitment.

TRADITIONAL	HCC
Status quo is accepted	Focused on continuous improvement
Reliance on extrinsic rewards (money, benefits, etc.) as a source of motivation	Fair extrinsic rewards exist, but intrinsic rewards (growth, recognition, etc.) are the main source of motivation.
Bosses are only interested in the employees' output.	Leaders genuinely care about and nurture the employee as a whole person.
Feedback is usually given only through formal systems.	Frequent informal feedback is provided between formal sessions.
Focused on what's not working and blaming those who are at fault	Frequent celebration of successes, and recognition of those who contributed to them
Scarcity mentality – Only so much to go around	Abundance mentality – There is plenty for everyone
Win – Lose	Win – Win
Bosses are feared	Leaders are trusted and respected
Assumption that people want to get away with doing as little as they can	Assumption that people want to contribute, learn, and grow
Conflicting signals and directives from bosses	Clear and consistent direction from leaders
Systems and policies are designed for the 5% who don't do the right thing	Guidelines are established for the 95% who want to do the right thing
Employees wait to be told what to do	Employees act on their ideas and initiate improvements
Reactive "Whack-A-Mole"-style fire fighting	Regular, proactive results reviews and action planning led by the people closest to the action

TRADITIONAL	HCC
Disagreements are frowned upon, and arguments are won by those in positions of power	Differences of opinion are celebrated and capitalized on to formulate better solutions
Focused internally and out of touch with the needs of the market or other stakeholders – Gradually irrelevant and suddenly extinct!	Focused externally and making improvements that make a difference for all stakeholders – Agile, competitive, and sustainable!

In my conversations and facilitated sessions I have not come across anyone who has found the descriptors under the *traditional* column to be very energizing or desirable. However, the issue is not that we don't agree that an HCC is more conducive to delivering, sustaining, and improving results, and makes for a much better work environment; the issue is that it takes commitment and intentionality to move the organization in that direction.

Many of these cultural attributes are interrelated and serve as both cause and effect of one another. The key is to identify a few of the attributes that would be critical to creating the culture you are after, and to make a commitment to do what needs to be done to fully implement them. Unfortunately, many organizations find themselves doing just enough to make it seem like they have embraced some aspects of this type of culture, but not enough to truly realize the benefits. When the going gets tough and the low-hanging fruit are picked, they fail to stay the course and move the organization beyond the tipping point. They end up creating what I call a "counterfeit HCC."

Sometimes, this happens merely out of lack of understanding. The leader may take a basic concept like "shared decision making" to the extreme and put every decision to a vote. The literal application of this concept could lead to an interpretation that an HCC is an absolute democracy and everyone has to be involved in every decision. This is where further coaching and calibration is needed to ensure leaders understand the true essence of the cultural attributes listed above.

On the other hand, there are times when the leader does not quite see the correlation between culture transformation and results, and is not willing, for whatever reason, to admit it. When this is the case, ill-fated and half-hearted attempts are made at implementing various aspects of the HCC but they do not yield the corresponding benefits. This can be damaging to the transformation process as it leads organizations to believe the HCC approach simply doesn't work for them. As a result, organizations end up in a state of confusion, as they know that the fundamental ideas behind an HCC are sound but they fail to see their practical benefits.

Some examples of the characteristics of counterfeit HCCs are shown below. As you go over the examples, assess your team or organization against these, and identify a few behaviors or cultural attributes that you are willing to commit to go after and transform:

Ideal: Stretching and energizing vision, shared by all team members
Opposite: No common vision
Counterfeit: Vision focused on solving a problem, not achieving something extraordinary

This type of vision does create a call to action, and it could invoke urgency and focus to solve a chronic problem, but the context it creates is one of survival and avoiding negative consequences, rather than inspiring the team to strive for what's possible. It is about working against something rather than for something. This counterfeit behavior can sometimes be remedied simply by replacing statements like "eliminate quality defects," with "deliver superior quality." However, the bigger issue is that this type of vision statement does not describe a vivid image of the desired outcome and it often only addresses a specific strategy or tactic that may or may not be sufficient to deliver that outcome. An example of this could be to "increase sales by 20%," when, in fact, the ultimate goal is to increase profitability to a certain level.

Ideal: Plenty of intrinsic rewards as the main source of motivation for team members
Opposite: Only extrinsic rewards
Counterfeit: Structured intrinsic rewards that create a win-lose culture

When recognition is formalized rather than being given in an authentic and spontaneous fashion, it begins to feel like leaders are doing it to check a box, rather than out of a genuine desire to express their appreciation. It also creates the perception that there is only so much recognition to go around and it causes people to be disappointed if they don't get their "fair share." Employee of the month programs are a good example of this as they are intended to recognize good performance but often generate far more dissatisfaction on the part of those who are not picked.

Ideal: Frequent informal feedback between formal sessions
Opposite: Heavy reliance on formal processes with no informal communication
Counterfeit: Watered down, inauthentic informal feedback

There is a good reason we have formal performance assessments and feedback sessions scheduled on a regular basis. These formal processes establish a minimum level of feedback that must be given with some frequency, but they must be supplemented with frequent informal feedback as well. If this informal feedback is not specific enough in content and authentic in delivery, it will leave the employee feeling devalued and unclear. This counterfeit HCC behavior is, at times, more damaging than not providing any feedback at all.

Ideal: Everyone engaged in meaningful work that impacts the results
Opposite: Active sabotage
Counterfeit: Most people actively criticizing each other, pretending they are concerned about the results

Organizations that tolerate gossip, and a "spectator" mentality and behaviors, perpetuate a perception that talking about problems and being dramatic about issues is a sign of concern and passion.

Ideal: Servant Leadership
Opposite: Dictatorship
Counterfeit: Benevolent dictatorship, paternal/maternal leadership

This type of leadership is usually practiced by bosses who have been in the same organization for years and have established unwritten rules of engagement that have everyone feeling like they are given freedom and authority, even though they know their decisions and actions had better fit into the range that the boss considers to be acceptable. Those who deviate from the established norms find themselves gradually irrelevant, and others fall in line knowing they will be protected as long as they don't challenge the boss' wishes.

Ideal: Engaged employees at all levels
Opposite: Disempowered and disengaged employees
Counterfeit: Everyone engaged but only the "in-crowd" engaged in meaningful work

> *There are a few "go-to" people for the important work. There is an appearance of engagement and involvement, but no real attempt to stretch others in the organization.*

Ideal: The people closest to the action making decisions
Opposite: Top-down decision making only
Counterfeit: A lot of people involved in giving input but decisions are not made in a timely manner

> *This is often a passive aggressive way to prove that getting the organization involved in decisions is counterproductive. Decisions are put to a vote when they shouldn't be, and indecision is attributed to a lack of consensus. The truth is that a real HCC is not a democracy and that not everyone always gets a vote on everything, but leaders who believe in the power of employee engagement figure out how to, sensibly, get the right people involved in the right decisions in a way that is productive, and it causes them to grow in their capability and commitment.*

Ideal: Everyone is a leader and has the necessary authority
Opposite: All authority is centralized
Counterfeit: Responsibility is given but not the authority, authority is accepted but not the responsibility.

> *This is all too common in the early phases of a transition to an HCC. The boss is willing to hold employees accountable for the results but is reluctant to give them the authority to make the decisions that impact those results. By the same token, employees tend to, at times, ask for*

the authority to make decisions when they may not have yet embraced the idea that there is a certain level of responsibility and accountability that comes with that authority.

Ideal: High trust
Opposite: Low trust
Counterfeit: Trust is extended only in low-risk situations

> *Leaders micro-managing their people when the stakes are high, rather than treating them like stewards and providing guidance, direction, and letting them get the work done.*

Ideal: Collaborative, multi-functional work teams
Opposite: People working in silos
Counterfeit: Integration happens only at the top of the organization, not among peers across silos

> *There is an expectation of allegiance to one's function rather than the broader team. Issues go all the way to the top for heads of functions to discuss and resolve them, rather than to people at all levels "reaching across the aisle" to come up with collaborative solutions.*

Ideal: Failures are treated as learning opportunities
Opposite: Mistakes are used to blame and punish people
Counterfeit: No real accountability for failures and no learning for the future

> *There is a general lack of accountability for the fear that holding people accountable may be perceived as anti-HCC. This results in failures being repeated, as their root causes are not identified and addressed.*

Considering what has been said so far about High Commitment Cultures, I believe you have a pretty good idea of what I consider to be a healthy culture that produces extraordinary results. I also trust that you have seen at least a few attributes of the culture that you consider to be impactful and capable of being leveraged in your environment. You may have found yourself wishing that your leaders would understand, and behave according to, these characteristics. If that is the case, I'd ask you to put yourself in their shoes, no matter where you are on the organizational chart, and consider these points from the point-of-view of someone who is responsible for instilling these cultural attributes in the organization.

In fact, the best way for you to be empowered to influence a transformation is for you, first and foremost, to consider yourself the one who is going to cause the culture shift to happen. I know this idea may seem daunting, depending on your level of experience or your perception of the power and authority you have in the organization. You may be correct in thinking that there is only so much you can do, but that is exactly where I want you to start. As you go through the rest of this book and become familiar with foundational principles of Transformative Leadership and the attitudes and actions of Transformative Leaders, focus on how they apply to you, not anyone else. Start right where you are and you'll be amazed how quickly your influence will grow.

Three Key Elements of Culture Transformation

One final point I'd like to make about culture transformation before we proceed, is that there are three key elements to transforming the culture of an organization that must be present in order to have any chance of success. They are as follows:

1. It is all about delivering and sustaining superior results

I know what you might be thinking. I have placed a great deal of emphasis on the value of culture and that seems to be contrary to this key element. Not really. Culture, or a set of behaviors that culminates in what we consider the culture of a team, is what produces the results. If you try to transform the culture as a social experiment without some stretching goals and an outcome that inspires the organization, the momentum cannot be sustained and ultimately, it won't work. Some of the ways the intent of this key element can be met are as follows:

A. Have a clear vision (results and cultural attributes) that leaders are committed to.

B. Have clearly articulated action plans, even though they will continue to evolve.

C. Have a robust review process to check progress and make adjustments.

D. Ensure that single-point accountability for the transformation resides with the leader, even though much of the authority should be shared.

2. Leadership capability is abundantly present at all levels

This is the one ingredient that makes everything else work. Without leadership capability, the organization will only get pennies on every dollar that is spent on systems and other improvements. Leaders must have:

A. Mastery of business processes, functional and technical systems, and the culture.

B. Mastery of Transformative Leadership and willingness to start with themselves.

C. Individual accountability for their own personal and professional development.

D. A Servant Leadership mentality, and the coaching skills that go along with it.

E. The courage to make bold choices and the commitment to implement them effectively.

3. *Culture transformation is an integrated approach, not a project*
While it is important to have clearly defined timelines, success criteria, and ownership of various aspects of the work, the work to transform the culture cannot be an independent set of interventions owned by a few people in the organization. It has to be built into everything we do across the organization:

A. Culture transformation is an integrated approach, not a set of tools or a standalone initiative.

B. Principles and methodologies of culture transformation are built into work processes, systems, and policies that deliver the results.

C. Organizational design features, such as structure, rewards, decision making, information sharing, and so on are holistically evaluated and modified to create the desired culture.

FOUNDATIONAL PRINCIPLES AND BELIEFS

I hope that, by now, you have some idea of the future state you are committed to creating. Can you envision the desired culture in your organization, the state of results it is delivering, the quality of interactions among team members, and all other pertinent aspects of your vision?

By far, the most important quality of Transformative Leaders is that they have seen what is possible in their mind's eye, and have such strong hunger for bringing it about that they remain 100% committed, regardless of how insurmountable the obstacles may seem.

There is absolutely nothing wrong with not knowing how you—or anybody else—would make that vision a reality at this point. The most important thing is to let your imagination, not your memories, shape your idea of what is possible. Let your confidence and faith in a brighter future, instead of the fear of the unknown or doubt in your abilities, fuel your imagination. No great social or technological breakthrough started with a crystal clear picture of how it was going to be achieved. None of those Transformative Leaders had the necessary tools and capabilities readily available from the start. The movements that endured and progressed against all odds did so because one person was clear about *why* the movements had to succeed, and their vision was taken up by a handful of people, then whole communities, and ultimately, nations.

At the risk of over-emphasizing this point, I would urge you, if you have not yet done so, to take some time to define the transformation you are committed to creating. No matter how large or small your vision is, I'd like you to not just describe it as if you were standing on the sidelines watching it happen, but as if you were participating in it. I'd like you to become familiar with what it feels like to be there. Set aside your concerns and doubts, if only for a moment, and create in reality the future

"Transformative Leadership is not about gaining more knowledge; it is about applying what you already know."

in your mind's eye that you would create if you had a magic wand. I'd like you to get in touch with the emotions this vision evokes in you, and truly recognize *why* it is important for it to become reality. This provides the basis for the rest of your journey as a Transformative Leader.

The remainder of this book will offer suggestions on *how* to transform the culture and results of your team into what you have envisioned. I will start by going over foundational principles and beliefs, then cover a number of One Point Lessons. My intention is to introduce you to a set of attitudes and actions for you to choose from and adopt, in order for you to be able to take full advantage of your insights.

Remember, Transformative Leadership is not about gaining more knowledge; it is about applying what you already know. You may find yourself revisiting the content of this book at various stages of your career to find that certain topics that didn't seem relevant before have taken on a whole new meaning.

"Do You Really Want It?"

Depending on your age and your interest in soccer, you may recognize this line from Ricky Martin's song, "The Cup of Life," which played on the radio hundreds of times during the 1998 World Cup competition. To be honest, I never paid much attention to the words in this song until I looked it up while writing this book. I have to say the message is quite profound, and it reminds me of one of the coaching techniques I have used over the years, as in the following example.

A few years ago, I met a woman at a manufacturing leadership event. We briefly spoke about the products and services that her company provided and exchanged contact information. At the end of the event, I ran into her again while we were both waiting in line for a taxi. After a few pleasantries, she came right out and shared with me that she was looking for a husband and had not been able to find one, divulging how her relationships would go only so far and then fizzle out. She asked me for coaching on the topic.

While I was no stranger to people approaching me for coaching, I was caught a bit off-guard this time. I started to say something funny like, "I am already married," but I sensed that this was no joking matter to her. I invited her to explain her situation, and when it was my turn to talk, as she looked at me with anticipation, I asked her why she didn't want to get married. I could tell she thought that I had misunderstood her, so she went on to explain that she did want to get married and repeated a few of her other points in case I had missed those too. After nodding my head and taking in everything she said, I asked her again to tell me why she didn't want to get married. At this point, it was clear to me that she was questioning her judgment about who she had chosen to approach for coaching. We talked for a few more minutes then parted ways as our taxis arrived.

A few weeks later, I received a phone call from an excited woman, telling me what a genius I was and thanking me. I didn't recognize the voice, so I asked who it was and sure enough, it was the same woman whom I had spent a few minutes coaching weeks earlier. She went on to inform me that she had discovered why she *didn't* want to be married. She said that she had been raised by her grandmother and had always spent holidays with her, and the main reason she was afraid of getting married was that she would have to spend some, or all, holidays with her husband's family. She was afraid that it would not be fair to her grandmother.

Now, I have no particular expertise in the art and science of finding a spouse, if there is such a thing. Although I have been happily married for a long time, I have no business giving anyone advice on how to find a life partner. However, it is clear to me that most of the time when we say we want something, but can't seem to acquire or achieve it, there is usually an underlying reason that we don't *really* want it. In my own experience, from my coaching conversations with others, I have always tried to get to this root cause and address it, rather than jumping into some formula or a set of steps that need to be taken. In the case of the woman I spoke of earlier, it wasn't clear to me why a host of eligible bachelors wouldn't be interested in a long-term relationship with her, but what had to be worked out first was her disempowering assumptions and her "either/or" mentality.

"The key is to be straight with yourself about what you want, and declare that commitment to yourself and others."

Is there something in your life, or career, that you say you want but have not been able to achieve? Ask yourself if you really want it. What would you have to give up in order to have what you say you want? What effort would you need to put in, and what risks would you need to take to have it?

According to Ricky Martin's song, "No one can hold you down, if you really want it!" We live in an era of instant gratification. We are used to everything being made easy for us, and why shouldn't we be? If it can be as easy as flipping a switch to turn on the heater versus having to go out, chop some wood and build a fire, more power to us. We should take advantage of it. However, if you are committed to causing a transformation, most of the easy stuff has already been done, and if you want to take it to the next level, it is going to take effort, sacrifice, and risk. In the words of Jim Rohn, "If you want something, you'll find a way. If you don't, you'll find an excuse."

The key is to be straight with yourself about what you want, and declare that commitment to yourself and others. Equally important is to be honest about all those things you say you want, but are not really committed to. Pretending that you are committed to something when you're not takes a lot of energy. Complaining without any real hope that the problem will ever go away mentally drains you. When you let go of your pretense, you recover energy that you can then channel toward things you really do care about and are committed to transforming.

If Only I Had a Time Machine!

I am fascinated with the idea of time travel. I have always been a big fan of the stories and movies on the subject. I often think about the implications of time travel being made possible and wonder if, at some point in the future, I will be able to visit my present-day self and give myself some advice. Wouldn't that be great?! Even better than that would be if I could use that time machine to go back a few more years and talk to the much younger version of myself. Boy, do I have a lot of wisdom to impart on that young fellow! Unfortunately, we don't live in "Fantasyland," and we can't do anything about what has already happened in the past.

I often ask the audience at my seminars and training classes what they think makes them the person they are at the moment, particularly referring to their attitude, and their enthusiasm or lack thereof. The resounding answer is always a list of people and events from their past; there is widespread consensus that all those things from our past shape our attitude in the present moment. Then, after they answer, I challenge this notion and set out to prove to them that the past actually has nothing to do with their worldview and attitude at that moment. So, let me have the same conversation with you, after a little anecdote.

A few years ago, my wife and kids and I took a nice three week vacation in Cancun. I had enough frequent flyer miles for one person, which had to be used to book a trip by a certain date, but travel could occur any time within the following 12 months. So, I went ahead and booked all four tickets for us to go to Cancun, one year in advance.

I would recommend this approach to anybody who is going to take a nice vacation because, during that entire year leading up to our vacation, the thought of being on the beach for three weeks kept me going. No matter what was going on, I was living into that future. It was almost like I got ten times my money's worth. On the other hand, I also remember the last few days of that vacation. Even though we had a great time for nearly three weeks and we were enjoying the beautiful weather and having a great time even in the last days, there was a cloud hanging over my head as I thought about leaving all of that behind and going back to work.

In both cases, it didn't matter how pleasant or unpleasant the past had been. It didn't even matter what was going on at the present. My attitude was determined by what I expected in the future, not by the past.

The reason most people believe that it is the past that shapes their attitude is that their perception of the future looks and feels suspiciously like their past. This is because we drag our past with us and project it into the future. The good news in all of this is that you don't need a time machine to change the past in order to get an entirely new attitude and alter the course of your future. All you have to do is set your sights on a better future and begin to act according to that future, instead of dragging around the same old stuff based on your past.

We have all experienced self-fulfilling prophecies whether we admit it or not. We predict an undesirable outcome, and the very thought of it happening drags us down and has us act according to the future that we don't want. Then when the very thing we predicted happens, we declare ourselves geniuses for having predicted it.

Let's say you are eager to get promoted and you get passed over. Based on that experience, you predict that you will never get promoted. That causes you to not go beyond the call of duty because, you reason, it wouldn't do any good anyway. That very behavior causes you to get passed over again, at which time, you proudly—and painfully—feel validated as a fortune-teller. This kind of thinking puts you in a vicious cycle of more of the past in your future, robbing you of your inspiration to change the trajectory of your destiny.

What if you changed this vicious cycle into a virtuous cycle in which you genuinely believed that, in spite of how things look, they will get better, and dwelled on that outcome and what it would feel like if it had already happened? This is what Transformative Leaders do. They believe in a transformation before they see evidence of it. Then slowly but surely, they begin to produce the evidence needed to get others on board, and when a whole lot of people believe in transformation, there is no stopping them.

If you subscribe to the idea that people's attitudes and actions are heavily influenced by what they expect in the future, then you would agree that most of us have the capacity to endure all kinds of adversity as long as we know the future is bright. It is when we give up hope that tomorrow will be better that we get exhausted and disappointed and act accordingly, only to seal the deal on our fate. If this is the case, how do you think people in an organization conclude what the future holds? By far, the most significant sources that indicate whether the future will be brighter or not are the attitudes and behaviors of the leadership team.

As a manufacturing plant manager, I experienced this all the time, but it took me several months to recognize what was going on. On some days, I'd walk out to the production floor and talk to people who were quite enthusiastic, and on other days, everyone seemed to be down. Once I recognized that they were simply mirroring my mood, I began to be a lot more conscious of the signals I sent to my organization.

Leaders are responsible for genuinely developing and believing in a vision of the future that inspires them and causes them to naturally spread enthusiasm about that future. I'm not talking about being inauthentic, although there will be times when you will have to "fake it 'til you make it," and spare people the gory details of all the things you don't feel great about. But for the most part, even if you have concerns about the way things are going, you can be straight about the situation, risks, and opportunities without coming across as a victim and shaking everyone's faith in a brighter future.

What future do you anticipate in the area in which you want to cause a transformation? Do you look to physical evidence around you to tell you what the future holds, or do you rely on your declarations? Are you driven more by the fear of the worst, or hope for the best? What signals are you sending to the rest of your organization about what the future holds?

"Every Organization is Perfectly Designed to Get the Results it Gets!"

This is a thought-provoking quote from Dave Hanna's book, *Designing Organizations for High Performance*. I don't know about you, but when things are not going well in my organization, the last thing I want to hear is that it "is perfectly designed to get the results it gets." There have been times in my career where I thought, "There is no way!" or, "What kind of an idiot would design an organization to have so many problems and deliver such mediocre results?" But the truth is that, whether someone consciously designed the organization that way or it happened by default, the current design is what is delivering the current results. If you want different results you have to "face the music," and take responsibility for changing something about the design.

Dave Hanna does a nice job of presenting a tool he calls the Organizational Performance (OP) Model in his book. The OP Model can be used to assess and design or re-design organizations for high performance. This assessment can be used to trace the organization's current results to its culture or behaviors exhibited within the organization. The behaviors can then be traced back to the culmination of the organizational design features such as structure, rewards, information sharing, decision making, and so on, and eventually to the business strategy that was behind those design features. The process of altering the culture, and therefore the results, of an organization involves questioning and modifying the strategy and/or the design features that are in place, such that the organization is designed to deliver different results than it is delivering today.

Are there gaps in your results? What behaviors or aspects of your culture are contributing to the gaps? What behaviors need to be different in your culture? Which of your organizational design features are causing unproductive behaviors to continue? Which design features need to be changed to expect and reward the desired behaviors, and to promote a different culture?

By diagnosing the root causes of the gaps you have in your results, you get to be intentional and make educated decisions about what steps you must take. Then, it is simply a matter of prioritizing the work and making it happen.

Why? Why? Why?

This takes me back quite a few years to when my kids were five or six years old. If you have ever been around little kids, I'm sure you know exactly what I'm talking about. They want to know the reason for everything and so their favorite question is, "Why?" And there seems to be no end to the string of "whys" they throw at you.

Of course, that's because they are trying to figure everything out, and thankfully, after a while the intensity of questions lessens, and eventually, they stop. Or do they? Actually, I don't think they do! I think we all stop asking "why" out loud at some point, but silently we go on asking "why." Then we come up with an answer based on whatever evidence we have gathered up to that point on the cause-and-effect relationships between things. We develop the ability to connect the dots and come to certain conclusions based on other knowledge we have gathered. As we do this, we get better and better at not just using the information that we have, but filling in the blanks with what we consider to be facts based on our experience. This is what I call putting 2 and 2 together and getting 5496!

I vividly remember coming home one day over twenty years ago and seeing my son, who was then a toddler, very excited to see me and trying, with his limited language skills, to convey what had happened that day. I remember him saying, "Guess where I *goed* today?" It was hilarious. I loved it. I almost didn't want to correct him because I was so excited that he had figured out the whole past tense thing.

Another time, my son and I were going somewhere in my truck and I was singing as I drove. I stopped and told him that I had a headache. He turned to me, in a very matter-of-fact way, and said, "I think your head hurts because you have been singing!" To this day, I am not sure if he truly believed there was a connection between the two events, or if he just wanted me to stop singing. I'd prefer to think it was the former, not the latter.

As adults, we continue to make cause-and-effect connections in our own mind when, in fact, some of the correlations we establish are about as unrelated as my singing and my headache. The trouble with this is that we look in the wrong places for the solutions to recurring problems, simply because we tend not to look beyond what we have always believed. Something happens and we immediately "know" why it happened *and* what needs to be done about it without the proper investigation to find the real cause. We form stereotypes and generalizations about people and organizations, and place blame because we know how *those people* are.

Are there problems about which you have recurring internal conversations? Have you stopped lately to re-examine your assumptions? Are your assumptions factual or are they stories you made up based on your past experience?

The 3 Cs of Success

I am a huge fan of Eckhart Tolle's work and his message about the power of being present. Unfortunately, most of us spend most of our time regretting the past and worrying about the future. If not to that extreme, we at least think about the past and the future enough that we are hardly ever present. Particularly, in this age of multi-tasking, we seem to always be distracted. This can have grave consequences, particularly because nothing ever happens at any other time than the present. You may disagree, but when all those things happened in the past, it was *now*. Whenever something happens in the future, it will be *now*. So, mastering the art of being in the present moment and making the most of it is paramount.

For a comprehensive study of this fascinating topic, I would refer you to Tolle's book, *The Power of Now*, which masterfully explores the idea of being present. I have listened to the audio book at least ten times, and something new has been revealed to me each time.

I'd like to introduce a simple method that will get you on your way to being present. The three Cs the title refers to are simply: *Complete Yesterday, Choose Today*, and *Create Tomorrow*.

Let's look at each of these in more detail:

Complete Yesterday – The main reason that we drag our past with us everywhere we go, and in some cases allow it to hinder new possibilities from showing up in our lives, is that there is something incomplete about it. An unhealthy relationship that we haven't quite come to terms with, the conversation we know we need to have but have been avoiding, the person we know we need to forgive but refuse to, and so on. Completing the past simply entails taking an inventory of the unfinished business that is pre-occupying us, and getting in action to complete it and clean it up so that we can be free from it. In some cases, this action may involve a conversation with someone, or some action taken toward something or someone, and in other cases, it may just involve letting something go and making the choice not to let it drag us down any more.

Create Tomorrow – I'd like to talk a bit about the future before we get to the present because, as we discussed earlier, the future that you create in your mind's eye plays a critical role in shaping your present state. Creating the future works best if it is done on a blank canvas rather than piled up on top of what is. I realize that you may not be able to completely transform everything, but if you are creating the future, you might as well define it exactly how you would want it, and then deal with the transition issues

65

later. Set yourself free from the constraints of the current circumstances and declare a bold future into existence. What if you can only get 80% of the way there? "The danger is not that we aim too high and miss. It is that we aim low and hit," to quote Michelangelo.

Choose Today – Now that you are free from the past and you know where you are going in the future, there is one more thing to do and that is to choose and accept today exactly as it is. We normally think of choice only being relevant when we have multiple options and we get to intentionally choose one over the other. When you go to the store to buy a dress or a suit, you get to examine your options and then choose one over the others. In that case, you will more than likely be happy with your choice, because you preferred it over the others you could have picked. What if you could choose any color car you wanted as long as it was black, as was the case when Henry Ford first came out with the Model T? If black were your favorite color, you would probably be happy, but if you wanted a red car, you'd be wondering why that choice was not available.

Reality is such that sometimes life deals us a hand that we don't necessarily want. This is when it becomes critical to play the hand that you were dealt, or make lemonade with the lemons you were given, and accept that it is what it is and deal with it! Unless you accept the way it is without complaining about it, you won't make progress toward how you want it to be. If you have a flat tire in the rain on the way to a wedding, choosing the present means you accept the present circumstances and get in action to change the tire, or call AAA, or whatever you have to do. The opposite would involve you kicking the tire and being angry and frustrated because you preferred the "no flat tire" option.

What derails our progress many times is not that we don't know where we are going, but that we don't like our starting point. We wish we were starting in a different place. It usually sounds something like this: I want to retire at 55 but I wish I had more money in the bank, or I want to start a new career but I wish I had more skills and resources, or I want to fly to San Francisco and I want to go there from New York but I'm in Atlanta.

The refusal to accept the current reality often keeps us from taking action; it keeps us stuck. The bottom line is that the only starting point you have is exactly where you are. Choosing today exactly as it is means you let go of what might have been and what could/should have been, and you go to work on how you can best go from exactly where you are to where you want to be.

None of this stuff is easy, and it requires commitment and discipline. It is also not a one-time shot. The minute you complete the past, more stuff starts creeping in. It is an ongoing endeavor, but if we accept it as a foundational principle, then we know it works if we work it. It comes down to accepting our current circumstances and living today as the beginning of tomorrow, not as an extension of yesterday. If you can do this all the time, you are a much better person than I am. I can tell you that most of us stumble and fall off

> *"The refusal to accept the current reality often keeps us from taking action; it keeps us stuck."*

the wagon, but as long as you remain committed to catching yourself deviating from this practice and getting back in the saddle, it works like a charm and brings peace and joy to your life.

There is no better time than now to examine how you're doing relative to the three Cs. Take some time now to identify a couple of opportunities to apply the three Cs and begin implementing them.

Who Do You Think You Are?

The answer to this question has a profound effect on the type and size of challenges you will take on in your career and in life. I am not asking this question in the context of your skills and experience or hobbies. The real question is: Who have you come to know yourself to be, as a person and as a leader?

If you know yourself as a person of integrity who follows through to make sure your commitment is delivered, you are more likely to play a bigger game in life. If you can count on yourself to hang in there when the going gets tough, you are much more likely to put yourself in situations that demand a lot of you, and are consequently more rewarding. If you know yourself as the opposite of the above, you will play small, as a person and as a leader.

I believe that we have all been created perfect, whole, and complete, and as we go through life, we have experiences that cause us to draw conclusions about ourselves, life, and the world around us. Unfortunately, most of these conclusions are not very positive and after a while, we cover up our empowered and energized self with a thick layer of limiting beliefs about ourselves. Not only that, but we also look for evidence to reinforce that we are not as smart as we should be, we can't be counted on, and so forth. We know every lie we have ever told and every bad thing we have ever done, and we begin to create an image of ourselves that is made up of all of that stuff.

After a while, when we look in the mirror, not only can we not see our empowered self, we forget it's even there. We see ourselves as the muck that has covered up our true self. This is evidenced by the fact that three-year olds are ever so enthusiastic about everything, they want to be and do everything, and 20 to 30 years later, not so much. Then, since we don't like what we see in the mirror, we try to cover it up with some icing. We put on a thin layer of pretense to make sure other people can't see what we consider to be our real self, which is really all the stuff we made up about ourselves over the years.

The worst part of this is that, after a while, you identify so much with who you think you are that you become protective and defensive, and refuse to even acknowledge your attitudes, actions, and habits that are not serving you or others well. This is only because you identify with those qualities as *you*. Otherwise you would be much more open to accepting feedback, and to objectively working to address your shortcomings.

Imagine that you put on an ugly mask and go to a costume party. If people laugh at your mask and talk about how ugly it is, you can laugh with them because you know the mask has no bearing on who you are, and in due time the mask will be taken off; it will have no power over you. But, if you forget that you have a mask on and you relate to that face as your own, you probably don't want to see yourself in the mirror, and you would certainly take offense if someone referred to your face as ugly.

There is much more to be said on this topic, but suffice it to say that the person you think you are is not capable of becoming a Transformative Leader. The good news is that you are not really who you think you are, and the real you that is underneath the layer of "muck" you put on is already a Transformative Leader. You see yourself as a hodgepodge of qualities you like and some that you don't. I want to show you that those three parts of you, the divine creation, the "muck," and the icing, are completely distinct parts, and only the divine part is the real you; the rest is the product of what has happened and the stories you have repeatedly told yourself about what happened.

The mere awareness of this concept, and the desire to distinguish the three distinct parts of yourself serve the purpose of enticing you to look for ways to neutralize the power the self-made part of you has over the real you. By doing this, you can gain access to the magnificent being that you inherently are. Much of the content of this book is aimed at causing you to discover the leader within you, rather than changing you into one. Even the slightest glimpse of your true self is enough to outweigh years of therapy and treatment to come to peace with the part of you that is made up of all the stories you have been telling yourself.

Your ability to be awesome does not depend on you denying the part of you that is not. In fact, just the opposite. When you acknowledge those other parts of you as something you have attached to yourself, rather than as your true self, you are more likely to authentically identify the attitudes and actions that are working against you, and be intentional about not allowing them to get in your way anymore.

Who you think you are determines the size of the challenges you will take on in your career and in life, and the size of those challenges creates a life that matches your expectations. Once again, it is a vicious cycle. The good news is that you can break that cycle and turn it into a virtuous one. What shapes your experience of life is a sum total of your thoughts, words, actions, habits, and character. Your life ultimately shrinks or expands to match the size of your commitments. When all you are focused on is survival, that is all you think and talk about, and your actions and habits all shrink to that level. When you set your mind on a stretching goal that you have many good reasons not to go after, your thoughts, words, and actions expand to fill the space you have just created.

There are several parts of this book that are aimed at assisting you in gaining access to the part of you that is capable of achieving the extraordinary in any circumstance. The key is to be open to the ideas, to receiving them, making them your own, and putting them into practice.

Be the Change...

The most important thing to remember in causing a culture transformation is that it is not about you changing anybody else. It is, as Mahatma Gandhi put it, about being the change that you want to see in the world. The question is not, "How am I going to change the culture?" but rather, "Am I willing to do what it takes to change *my* behavior in a way that compels others to choose to change theirs?" We all know that on some level, but everyone is waiting for someone else to go first!

Culture change can happen in an instant if everyone makes the choice to adopt a different set of attitudes and behaviors. An example of instantaneous culture change is when disaster strikes. Priorities become crystal clear in an instant and everybody is singularly focused on a common goal and working in concert with others, rather than being stuck on criticizing and complaining.

Unfortunately, most of us spend the majority of our time thinking about and doing things that make no difference in the grand scheme of things because we, individually or as an organization, do not

> *"What distinguishes Transformative Leaders from others is their willingness to go first."*

71

have a compelling need and vision that inspires us to think or do otherwise. Then, when we see that no progress is being made, we look for the cause in all the wrong places, blame the culture, other people, our bosses, or the government. The key is to make a personal choice to role model the change, and thus inspire others to do the same. If enough people declare themselves, individually, the cause of the current culture, and unconditionally commit to a different behavior, we can shift the culture instantly. What distinguishes Transformative Leaders from others is that they are willing to go first while everyone else is waiting for a critical mass to agree with the direction.

This is particularly important in this day and age, when the rate of change is mind-boggling, particularly to those of us who grew up in another generation. Success and, I dare say, survival in today's economy depends on our ability to adapt and change at unprecedented speed. It is no longer a luxury and a competitive advantage, but rather a matter of survival, to constantly evaluate our culture and master the art of transforming it, starting with ourselves.

Theory X, Theory Y

Do you know people in your organization who are just lazy? I mean the ones who avoid responsibility at all cost and don't want to take any initiative. They want to do the minimum to get by. They are known in some circles as the ones who want to "do their eight and hit the gate!" I know you can think of at least one person who is that way, right?

When I ask this question at my workshops, just about everybody raises their hand with much enthusiasm. Of course, then I ask the next question, which I'd like to pose to you: Are you one of those people? As you can imagine, I hardly see any hands go up. Nobody is willing to label themselves as a generally demotivated and lazy person. Somehow, although there is always a widespread belief that those lazy people are out there, they hardly ever end up in my workshops. This is particularly disappointing because I know those people would benefit from the stuff I talk about in my sessions!

Let me ask the question differently. What if I asked you if you sometimes behave like those lazy people? Are you ever just frustrated, demotivated, and want to get by with doing the minimum? Again, my experience from my workshops has been that most people admit that sometimes they behave that way, which begs the question: Why didn't they raise their hands when I asked them if they were lazy and demotivated? The answer is very simple. It is because we judge ourselves by our intentions, and everyone else by their behavior. When we behave badly, we have plenty of justifications, but when others do the same, we label them as lazy. Of course, as a leader, your perception of whether your employees are motivated or not has a profound effect on how you will treat them, and as a result, how you go about addressing organizational issues.

Douglas McGregor, professor of management at the MIT Sloan School of Management in the 1960s, frames this phenomenon as "Theory X and Theory Y" in his book, *The Human Side of Enterprise*. McGregor's "Theory X" assumes that people are lazy and they don't want to take initiative, and "Theory Y" suggests that people are generally good and they want to contribute, and so on. The truth is that most of us find ourselves having some good days and some bad days for a variety of reasons, and we also know people who gravitate more toward one end of the spectrum or the other.

The issue is not whether we can reach consensus on all people being good or bad. The question is what approach you will take when someone is not performing to their potential or they seem to be disengaged? Is your tendency to assume that it is because they are simply lazy, and look no further to understand the underlying cause of the issue? Or are you inclined to assume that the person wants to be a part of something significant, and like you, he/she also wants to contribute, but something is in the way?

Transformative Leaders tend to take the latter approach and ask themselves what they can do to create the conditions in which the person will flourish and express their leadership and potential. This doesn't mean you let people off the hook. On the contrary, if you are truly accountable for creating the right environment in which people perform, you recognize and act upon your responsibility to follow up on performance outages, and occasionally, you may even end up making a decision to terminate someone's employment. But, if it gets to that point, you will know—and the person will also know and appreciate—that you treated them with respect and dignity every step of the way, as you coached and counseled them and looked for ways in which they could be extraordinary. In the end, everyone must make choices and be accountable for the consequences. Transformative Leaders don't allow their experiences with the few who make bad choices cause them to paint everyone with the broad brush of laziness, and they don't let themselves off the hook.

The implications of "Theory X and Theory Y" go way beyond managing performance. Whether you subscribe to one or the other impacts your decision to set your policies with the 1-2% of abusers in mind, or the other 98% who are honest. It also determines whether the continuous improvement processes and systems you use to learn from mistakes turn into a company-sanctioned witch hunt, or remain focused on improving work processes to prevent problems in the future.

Which theory do you subscribe to? Are you willing to take at least partial, if not full, responsibility for the worst performer on your team? If so, what steps could you take to create the conditions that are conducive to that person getting energized?

Integrity is Everything!

Do you examine every chair that you sit in, or do you just assume it will hold your weight? Do you go through an intersection when your signal is green, or do you stop to make sure the cars crossing the traffic don't run the red light and hit your car? Do you personally examine the airplane before a flight, and make sure that the pilots are sober and competent before you fly, or do you place your trust in the processes that are in place to make sure you get to where you are going safely?

When you place your trust in an object, a person, or a process, you are in fact counting on it performing according to its stated purpose or function. If the integrity of the chair is not compromised, it will perform per design and hold your weight. Likewise, if someone has given you their word on a certain topic, and their actions and results match what they promised, then they are in integrity and you are more likely to trust them even more. If someone has honored their word consistently, you are more likely to trust them. If they repeatedly say one thing and do another, you would begin to question their integrity. The obvious consequence of you behaving as a person of integrity is that others will trust you. But, the most profound impact of your integrity has nothing to do with other people. The most important impact is whether or not you can count on the creative power of your own word.

If you can count on yourself to keep your word, you make bold declarations, believe in the future you declared, and follow through with making it happen. If you have come to know yourself as a person who says one thing and does another, then you don't trust yourself. There are many ways in which you can protect your integrity and restore it on an ongoing basis. Honoring your word is a huge one. Chances are, if you are up to something big in life, you won't be able to keep all the promises you make; but honoring your word means you communicate that you won't be able to keep your promise and work out a mutually acceptable agreement that keeps you in integrity.

When you cut corners and do not perform a task as it should be done, even if no one else finds out, you have chipped away at your integrity in your own eyes, and that is enough to do damage to your ability to count on yourself to deliver. Sometimes, we dismiss a lack of integrity in our life as something "minor" and we trivialize the damage it does. I am fairly certain that if the word got out that only 99% of a certain airline's pilots were properly trained, and only 99% of the time they were sober when they flew the planes, that airline would not be in business for long. Yet we think it is okay to be five to ten minutes late to meetings without communicating. We think it is fine to only follow through on 75% of the commitments we have made and so on. We think 90% is good enough because we have learned that 90% integrity, or sometimes much less, is good enough to produce the kind of success we have achieved in our lives. But this conversation is not about what you have accomplished *so far*, it is about what you believe is possible in the future.

If you are content with maintaining the status quo, this topic may not be relevant to you, but if you are truly interested in taking it up a few notches and going for the gusto, then you have to know that what has gotten you here won't necessarily get you to where you want to be. You see, you have already figured out what chances you are willing to take, and how big a game you want to play in life, based on what you think you can be counted on to deliver. If you want to take bigger chances where the stakes are high, you must start with yourself and restore your integrity to build a solid foundation for the bigger game you want to play in life.

Overall, it is not the immediate impact of a broken promise, a late arrival to an appointment, or partial completion of a task that does the damage. It is the collective image that it creates of us, as a leader with no integrity, in the eyes of others and, more importantly, in our own eyes, that over time renders us irrelevant.

Where are some places where you are out of integrity, where your words and actions don't line up? What are you willing to commit to do to restore your integrity, and to begin to behave differently? Are you willing to be authentic about your discovery and publicly declare your intentions to behave differently in the future, or be straight about your lack of commitment and accept the consequences?

I Am "The One" and It's Not About "Me"

This statement sums up the essence of Servant Leadership, which is a key characteristic of Transformative Leaders. The two components in this statement work together to create a powerful mindset for a leader. When you declare yourself "The One," you don't do it because you have an illusion that you have control over everything. You do it because you are saying, "If it is to be, it's up to me!" You are embracing your responsibility, giving up your excuses and the right to pass the buck. The only thing better than being "The One" is recognizing, at the same time, that whatever happens in the process of you fulfilling your commitment is not about you. The recognition that it's not about you keeps you from constantly focusing on trying to protect yourself and your interests at the cost of your team/organization.

If you are "The One" and it is *all* about you, you behave like a bully and dictator. If you get that it's not about you but you don't think you're "The One," you act like a victim. You don't have to look far to find so-called "leaders" who fit in to either of these categories. It's easy to be an overbearing boss who thinks it is all about them and that everything has to go through them because they are in charge. It is also easy to fall into the trap of being too nice and not really providing the

> *"A leader cannot truly be 'The One' if he/she thinks it is all about him/her."*

kind of leadership that people deserve. When you embody both parts of this seemingly paradoxical statement at the same time, you unleash a brand of empowerment in yourself and others around you that can move mountains. I submit that a leader cannot truly be "The One" if he/she thinks it is all about him/her. I propose that the only way to be a true leader is to embrace both concepts simultaneously.

Do you behave in a way that clearly lets your employees know that you take full responsibility for the team's results? Do you embrace your responsibility in a way that makes it evident that it is about the vision and not you? If you are out of balance on either side, what can you do to take a more balanced approach and practice both concepts?

Don't Just Kill the Weeds! Feed the Grass!

My wife and I live in Atlanta, Georgia where we thankfully don't experience long winters. Regardless, our grass does turn brown and stops growing for a couple of months every year. Every Spring for the first few years after having moved, we would talk about how we needed to put down some pre-emergent so that the weeds wouldn't come back next year, as they normally did, way before the grass started growing. For some reason it never got done. Every year in the Spring, we would scramble, trying to spray weed-killer, but that stuff never quite did the trick. I am happy to say, though, that as soon as the grass started growing, it would choke out the weeds and we would be 90% free of weeds for the growing season.

I learned an important lesson from this experience. Namely, that the same concept applies to cultures. You can either chase the aspects of the culture that you don't like and try to squelch them, or you can accentuate the positive and let the positive aspects of your culture choke out the negative. That is not to say that it is not appropriate to sometimes uproot a dandelion that is sitting in the middle of your beautiful lawn. Of course, there are instances where you must directly deal with certain behaviors or norms that, if ignored, would severely hinder progress. But in most cases, it is cultivating the right behaviors and catching people doing something right that does more for perpetuating the desired culture than going after everyone who is doing wrong.

ONE POINT LESSONS

Don't Settle for Just "Managing Change!" Take On "Leading a Transformation!"

"The secret to change is to focus all of your energy, not on fighting the old, but on building the new." - Socrates

Good leaders are great at *change management,* but great leaders don't stop there. They go way beyond managing change, they *lead transformations.* The difference between *managing change* and *leading a transformation* goes far beyond simple semantics.

For the purposes of this book, I'd ask you to consider that "transformation" is different from "change," just as "leadership" is different from "management."

- Change starts with something we don't like. As we try to change what we don't like, we meet all kinds of resistance because of the beliefs we have always had.
Transformation inspires us to influence our environment and go for something big rather than just tweaking what we don't like.

- Change acts on us. Transformation causes us to act on our current circumstances.

- Change is reactive. Transformation is proactive.

- Change is short-term focused. Transformation often produces immediate results, but in the context of what matters most in the long run.

- Change starts from the outside and is often forced upon us. Transformation starts from the inside and it is often driven by us being inspired by what's possible.

To illustrate these distinctions, I'd like you to consider that, whereas change starts with "what is" and attempts to keep what is working intact and eliminate what is not, transformation simply starts with "nothing" and is led by a vision of the whole as if it were to be created from scratch today. The former views today as an extension of yesterday and tries to make the most of what is. The latter sees today as the beginning of tomorrow and shapes today's circumstances as a solid foundation for what will be.

Change often results in unexpected, or in some cases, known and tolerated, side effects that create other problems. Would you believe the main motivation for inventing cars was to eliminate "pollution" caused by horse droppings that were becoming an increasingly annoying problem in the streets? Yes, there were many positive benefits that came out of this invention, such as enabling people to travel long distances in shorter periods of time, but cars were invented to solve a pollution problem! How do you think we did? ...Exactly! We solved the original problem and created a bigger one.

A more recent illustration of this concept is the prevalent use of medication or other medical treatments that solve one problem and create multiple new ones. If you don't know what I'm talking about, next time you watch a prescription drug commercial on TV, pay close attention to the disclaimers they go over at the end. Some of the side effects of the drugs being advertised are far worse than the problems they are supposed to solve. They tell you a certain drug will cure your migraine headaches but in the end they warn you that taking the drug could cause suicidal thoughts and/or increase your chances of a heart attack by 50%! Now, I am not against taking some pain medication now and then, but let's agree that the main cause of a headache is not aspirin deficiency. A transformative approach to health may involve some steps to experience temporary relief from some of the symptoms, but it goes beyond that and serves the purpose of creating total wellness and vitality.

The same is true in organizations. Leaders often identify and address symptoms of problems they see, but fail to take a holistic approach in transforming the organization's results and capability to create a sustainable step change. I am inviting you to consider that, while transforming the state of any organization certainly does involve dealing with today's problems, whether or not a lasting transformation is achieved depends greatly on how we view our role as leaders and whether or not we embrace the full scope of *leading a transformation* instead of just *managing change.*

This is not to invalidate what we know and love about change management in a traditional sense. In fact, you will see traces of the principles and methodologies of change management throughout this book. However, it is my intention for you that by applying the principles and adopting the approaches presented in this book, your capacity to transform your organization's results and its ability to sustain and improve those results will significantly increase to levels that you never thought possible.

Now, let's examine a bit more closely the characteristics of transformation and how it might differ from the approach most leaders take most of the time. Over and over again, in my coaching practice, I have come to find that when someone is dissatisfied with their current circumstances and is asked about the outcome they are ultimately after, they immediately begin to talk about what they don't like about their current situation. In other words, if someone handed them a magic wand they would immediately wish their problems away rather than ask for the perfect outcome that they want.

Change versus Transformation

Change focuses on solving today's problems and trying to avoid the default future.

Transformation focuses on achieving the milestones necessary to create the designed future.

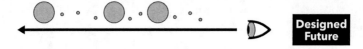

As illustrated in the figure above, the "change" model involves us standing in the present, looking out at a better outcome at some point in the future. In the present, we are far more clear about the problems that need to be solved and actions that we must take to solve them, than we are about what that desired future looks like or what major milestones must be achieved for that outcome to come to be. I see this all the time with top executives of major corporations as I speak at leadership summits in the US and abroad.

I take the audience through an exercise titled "Transformation Blueprint"—which we will discuss in more detail in the section titled "Final Thoughts"—and I ask them a few simple questions, starting with, "What area of your business are you out to transform?" and, "What will it look like when you are there?" I invariably see these directors, VPs, and C-suite executives in deep thought, trying to figure out the answers to these questions. It is obvious to me, looking at the faces of two to three hundred people, that 80% of them have no idea how to answer these questions. This is not to say that they can't list the goals and targets they are aiming to achieve; I am sure every one of them would get writer's cramp if I asked them to write down all the problems they needed to solve. If you happen to be one of these folks, I want you to know you're not alone. I am not trying to condemn you, but rather compel you to recognize what is going on and to deliberately adopt a different approach.

Most of us are wired to automatically think in terms of what we don't want, rather than to think about the perfect outcome we are committed to creating. The good news is that once you become aware of this automatic process and take a few simple steps to condition your thought process in a different direction, you very quickly set yourself, your organization, and your results apart from your peers who have not taken the time to be deliberate in doing so.

In contrast with the "change" model, the "transformation" model involves stepping out into the future, independent of today's reality and defining, in as much detail as possible, what the desired future looks like, *and then* identifying the key milestones that must be achieved and conditions that must be created in order for that future to manifest in reality. Then, after the future has been defined and the milestones identified, we still have to deal with our current reality. Yes, you will still have problems to solve, but as a Transformative Leader, everything you do will now be done in the context of creating the desired future and making sure that the critical milestones are reached.

You will have setbacks and you'll re-prioritize along the way, but you will have a much better chance of achieving extraordinary results by taking this approach.

My personal experience with this is that a few years ago, following a transition in my career, I found myself leading a manufacturing plant that was the worst in the entire company. For months, I made virtually no real impact by trying to identify all the things that needed to be fixed and assigning them to people. I couldn't see the needle moving significantly on any front. It seemed like we were in a never-ending game of "whack-a-mole." Then I finally realized that I needed to take a different approach. I needed to set a stretching goal that would transform our reality, as opposed to trying to solve one problem at a time, hoping to survive. So, I created a vision for the plant to become "The Showcase of Excellence," which was a phrase I borrowed from a colleague I had worked with many years earlier.

Well, this changed everything—for me that is—but it still had no real impact on everybody else. While I was going around telling people about my vision for the plant, they looked at me like I had two heads. Instead of trying to understand why they were not as excited as I was, I resorted to self-righteousness and blaming them for not having any interest in transformation. Fortunately, through a series of steps I took to figure out how to get myself out of the way of progress, I realized that not only did they have no clue what "The Showcase of Excellence" would look like, neither did I. Then, one day, I got my leadership team together and we had an open conversation about this vision and what it would mean, and we made a very specific list of 11 items that described the results and the culture and dynamics, and so on, in a way that got us all excited about making it happen.

That was the day that we truly committed ourselves to where we were going. We still had no idea how to overcome our barriers and the challenges we would face along the way but, we were committed to making it happen. Less than two years later, against all odds, the plant was delivering benchmark results and managed to maintain a #1 ranking for the next few years.

I am positive that you can relate to everything you have read so far as something that makes sense in theory—at least I hope. You might even feel you could potentially apply it to yourself and your situation, but then there are those "yeah buts," and what you do with them determines whether this book will transform your leadership effectiveness or if it will just arm you with some good information and perspective. The latter is nice but it falls far short of my hopes and dreams for what you will get out of reading this book.

This is where the road splits and you must make a decision about which way you are going to go. Remember, I already told you that your transformation will not come from what I tell you, but from what you tell yourself and ultimately what you do. You could let your objections get the best of you—and I'm sure you will have plenty of justification to do so. Those objections are what always keep us from trying a new approach, which in turn keeps us stuck in the same old patterns we say we want out of. I'd urge you to let your doubts and concerns just be there; you don't have to get rid of them or wonder why they are there. Don't over-think it. Just get in action on the insights you receive and do your best to stay in action.

The Bottom Line:

Managing change is good for fixing and improving some aspects of the current circumstances. This is often sufficient to produce the results we are looking for, but it doesn't carry the day when we intend to create a step change. Leading a transformation involves change, but it starts with the desired future and gives the leader a whole new perspective.

 ## Reflection Questions:

1. Do you operate in the "change" mode or "transformation" mode most of the time?

2. What area of your business (or life) do you want to transform? Pick one area and be specific.

3. What tangible results will be achieved when the transformation has taken place? State the specific, hard number results.

4. What qualitative results will be achieved when the transformation has taken place? State the benefits that you may not be able to express in hard number results. Describe the environment and behaviors and attitudes of the people involved.

5. Looking back from the transformed future, what key milestones or achievements do you see that must happen along the way? Approximately, by when should they be achieved? Just capture these based on what you know and be okay with modifying them as you move forward.

6. Are you genuinely excited about what you are about to create? If not, your vision is not big enough.

7. Do you know exactly how to go about creating the transformation? If so, your vision is not big enough.

8. Who are the key people who need to be committed to the vision? What specific actions will you take, and by when will you take them, to get others energized about the idea?

Recommended Follow-up Action:

1. Commit to transforming something in your life and use the answers to the above questions to get started.

2. Share your idea with others and get them energized by the possibility of it coming to fruition.

3. Make public declarations and put yourself on the hook to deliver your transformation.

4. Use the transformation that you have chosen to work on as the context for this book. As you read, look for insights on how you might accelerate progress by applying the insights that are revealed to you.

You are Looking for the Key in the Wrong Places

"People often ask me, 'How do you grow an organization?' Very simply, grow yourself." - John Maxwell

I once read a story about a man who was out at night, in the street, searching for something. Someone passing by stopped and asked him what he was doing, and the man said he had lost his keys and was looking for them. The stranger offered to help him find his keys and joined him in the search. After several minutes of searching and not finding anything, the stranger asked the man when he noticed he lost his keys, hoping to find some clues as to in which direction to expand the search. In response, the man said that he was walking home and noticed that he didn't have his keys a few blocks up. Bewildered at the response, the stranger asked, "Why are you looking here when you know you lost the keys somewhere else?" The man answered, "Because the street where I think I lost my keys is too dark and this is the first street light I saw, so I figured I'd be better off looking here because there is more light and I can see better!"

I'm sure it is abundantly clear that this approach makes no sense and the keys would never be found. I am also certain none of us would ever do something like this, but you may be surprised at how many times you engage in the same practice and don't recognize that you are simply looking for the key where it is convenient to look, not necessarily where you might find it. Where the light is shining is "out there," on the circumstances and other people. That is usually the first place we go to find solutions to our problems. When things are not working out or we are not delivering the results we would like to deliver, we get into a cycle of finding something wrong with the way things are or what other people are doing or not doing, and we fail to look at how our own thought processes or behavior might be contributing to the problem. In other words, we refuse to take responsibility for our part in creating the situation we are in. We get fixated on people and things we don't have control over and we remain in victim mode.

I want you to consider that the first decision you must make after you get clear on what it is you are out to transform is that you are the greatest barrier to progress, and then you must go to work on getting yourself out of the way. I am not suggesting you ignore the problems you need to solve in order to achieve the results. On the contrary, I want you to tackle those problems with absolute courage and determination. What I am suggesting is that the best way to do that powerfully is to understand what is holding you back from hitting the problem with all you have. It is definitely okay to look out there for what actions need to be taken and what barriers must be addressed in order to make progress, but those are all primary causes of lack of progress. The "root cause" is often hidden in places where it might be harder to look, such as the way you have responded to the situation.

Once you know enough about the results you are out to achieve, and have identified the key milestones you must reach along the way as well as the forces that are acting against progress "out there," it is time to be straight with yourself about whether your thought processes and actions are working for you or against you. This is where you will find the real key to progress.

The Bottom Line:

We often look in convenient places for solutions, which are not necessarily where we might find them. Self-awareness in discovering how we contribute to the very circumstances we don't want to have in our lives is the toughest, but most powerful way Transformative Leaders find the key to permanent shifts in their effectiveness.

Reflection Questions:

1. Do you have any recurring complaints about a problem you have not been able to solve?

2. How long have you been tolerating the problem? Why?

3. What is the most important step you could take to resolve the problem or influence someone who can?

Recommended Follow-up Action:

1. Think of a specific area of work or life that is not going well.

2. Make an inventory of the most common recurring complaints you have about what is in the way of progress.

3. Identify what you have done to contribute to them and why you have been tolerating them.

4. Identify 1 to 2 actions you are willing to take in the next 24 hours and make a commitment to get in action.

5. Make it a habit of asking yourself, "Why do I tolerate that?" often when it comes to problems you encounter, and look inward for the answer.

LESSON 3

Transformative Realizations Have an Expiration Date!

"It is not enough to have knowledge, one must also apply it. It is not enough to have wishes, one must also accomplish."
- Johann Wolfgang von Goethe

Over the years, I have had the privilege of coaching a variety of people from all walks of life and all kinds of backgrounds. I can honestly say that the ones who have produced the greatest tangible benefits in things that mattered to them have been the ones who had had very little exposure to self-help books, classes, and that sort of thing. They are the ones who get excited about taking their insights for a test drive and put them into action immediately.

The ones who struggle are those who are more sophisticated; they are the ones who have read books and attended classes. They get engaged in conversations but in the back of their mind they are thinking, and sometimes they say, "I already know this stuff but it hasn't worked for me." Therefore, they are reluctant to put much effort into doing the work to experience the manifestation of what they already know in their lives. What they fail to realize is that, as Tony Robbins says, "it is not *knowing* what to do, but *doing* what you know," that gets results.

I know this feeling very well from my own experience. I once set a goal to run a marathon. This would represent a huge breakthrough in my life because, literally, all my life I had not been able to run for more than a few minutes without getting winded and thoroughly exhausted. In my quest to become a runner, I researched books on running and bought one that several people recommended and started reading it. Several weeks later, I knew a lot more about diet and exercise routines, but concluded that the book was not all that great because it didn't really help me. So I set the book aside and figured I would never be able to run.

Before I bought that book, I had some hope that maybe if I learned something about training myself I would be able to break this 50-year cycle and actually be able to run, but after my experience with the book I was convinced that I would never be able to achieve my goal. I know what you're thinking and you're right: It turns out, to become a runner, you have to actually get out there and run. Knowledge helps, but only if you do the work, and I didn't.

Likewise, when you get hold of a transformative realization, you have to use it right away or else it will not only not do you any good, it will also set you back in your journey. Just like any fresh produce that you buy at the store, your transformative realizations lose their flavor over time and eventually spoil and become useless. If you put them to use immediately, you begin to see benefits and they will produce new realizations; as long as you continue to stay in action and put your insights into practice, they are gifts that will keep on giving. But after a certain period of *knowing* something and not *doing* anything

> *"It is not knowing what to do, but doing what you know."*
> *- Tony Robbins*

with it, when someone coaches you, you will say, "I know, I know!" as if knowing something is supposed to miraculously produce benefits.

The other side effect of going after self-awareness but not taking action is that it creates a sense of dissatisfaction that wasn't there before. Let's say you have lived a sedentary life, you are not physically fit, and every night you go home, and eat some potato chips and ice cream in front of the TV. Then you get exposed to some information and come to realize that you are actually doing your body harm, and that unless you begin to act differently, you will soon develop health issues and so on. Having this information is a good thing, but only insofar that it spurs you to act. Otherwise, now that you know about the perils of your lifestyle, you can no longer enjoy your ice cream and potato chips the way you used to. At least before, you were enjoying yourself, but now even that has been taken away from you.

I believe I can say with confidence that every one of us has a list of things that we know we ought to do, which we are not doing. So, if you are feeling condemned or making yourself wrong, please recognize that you are not alone and you certainly are not a bad person. You are just a person. There is nothing you can do about the way you have behaved in the past, but the great news is that there is a whole lot you can do about how you are going to behave in the future, and answering the questions at the end of this section, in addition to getting in action with the follow-up, will get you on the right track.

By the way, I am happy to say that while it has been about five years since I bought the running book, I finally did get in action and ran my first 5K in 2014, and I plan to run many more in the future. I am now a runner, thanks to my daughter who gave me the much needed nudge by signing me up for the 5K as my Father's Day gift.

The Bottom Line:

*Knowing what to do makes no difference so long as you don't **act** on what you know. Acting on new knowledge when it is acquired provides evidence of how it can be useful, and it keeps us in action. Filing new knowledge in the "someday" category causes us to lose faith in whether or not that knowledge is of any use to us.*

Reflection Questions:

1. Have you ever responded with an, "I know, I know," when somebody gave you some good advice or coaching, as if to dismiss the idea?

2. Do you have a long list of things that you are hoping to get around to doing "someday?"

3. Do you read books and go to classes to pick up head knowledge, and then not put what you learned into practice in your life?

4. Have you become cynical and resigned about doing things you know you ought to do to restore your physical, emotional, social, or financial well-being?

Recommended Follow-up Action:

1. Starting right now, when you hear or read a message that you have come across before, and your mind begins to take you to the place of, "I have heard this before," as a way to escape having to take action, intentionally look at aspects of your life where that message applies at that moment and explore what commitments you are willing to make. Get in action while the noise is going on in the back of your mind.

2. Think of 3 to 5 specific things that you have recently realized about yourself that you would like to act upon and have not yet done so.

Now, either choose to let them go and forgive yourself for not having done anything with them, or commit to some action you are going to take by a certain date that will get you in action or back in action.

3. As you read the rest of this book, make it a point to either act on the points that resonate with you right away, or accept that you are not yet ready to take action and move on. Whatever you do, don't put anything else on your "someday" list. You can always pick up the book and go through some of the points and perhaps find that something else resonates with you at that moment in your life. Remember: When the student is ready, the teacher will appear, so don't worry about missing out.

Life Lessons from a GPS!

"We may encounter many defeats, but we must not be defeated."
- Maya Angelou

I am convinced I was born with a part of my brain—that one that helps you find your way around—completely missing, and that my condition is exacerbated when my wife is riding in the car with me. She is the absolute opposite of me and always tells me which way to go—most of the time, right before I miss my turn! It's like she has some sort of built-in radar and always knows the way. For years, she had to navigate most of the way as I drove us to her dad's. For some time, she was convinced that it was just because I didn't want to go there, until it became painfully obvious that physical directions are not my thing.

I was so glad when we moved to Germany and both of our cars had built-in GPS systems installed. I never had to worry about getting around. Of course, the drawback was that if I ever wanted to go somewhere I had been several times, I still had to get the GPS to tell me which way to go since it was too easy for me to just follow orders and not register the turns in my mind.

Although my wife is one of the most patient people I know, one marked difference between her, the human GPS, and the electronic one is that she has certain expectations of me to remember simple routes and make the correct turns without being instructed, while the electronic GPS couldn't care less. On several occasions as my wife assumed I knew which way I was going, only to experience yet another wrong turn, we would get into arguments about why it was that I still couldn't remember how to get there and so on. However, the GPS is always cordial and polite, and even when I don't follow her instructions, she immediately recalculates the route and tells me what my next turn is to get myself back on track. All of this is always done without a trace of sarcasm, frustration, or disappointment. I have never heard my GPS say, "I told you to make a right turn! Why did you miss that turn?" or, "I can't believe you did that! Now it is going to take you five more minutes to get there!"

Wouldn't it be great if we lived our lives that way? Think about it. The GPS only cares about one thing, and that is to get you to your destination in the most efficient way possible. In doing so, the GPS considers only two pieces of information. The first, is where you are going, and the second, where you are now. It then calculates what your next, best move ought to be. It never looks back and spends any time on what could have or should have been in the past, or the potential impact that the wrong moves made on the future.

What if we could put all of our focus and energy on identifying, and acting on, the next, best move we ought to make to get to where we want to go from where we are now? What if we could stop regretting the past and wondering how much further along we would have been had we not made those wrong turns? What if we stopped over-analyzing all the "what if" scenarios and accepted our current position as the only starting point we have? What if we acted with courage in the face of uncertainty, knowing that if it didn't work out, we could make more course corrections and get there eventually?

The best example of this that I have seen in a human being, albeit a fictional one, is Forrest Gump. If you have seen the movie, or better yet, read the book, you know that Forrest accomplished more in his lifetime than most of us dream of, in spite of the fact that he wasn't exactly the sharpest tool in the shed. That was because he didn't over-think things like most of us do. He got clear on where he was going and what had to be done, and he did it, one step at a time.

If you're like me, you have plenty of thoughts that are rolling around in your head about what you could have or should have done differently. How about committing to living your life like the GPS and staying focused on where you are going, accepting where you are now as an unchangeable fact, and diverting all of your energy toward what step you must take next?

 The Bottom Line:

Progress is a function of knowing where you are going and taking the very next step that will move you in the direction of that destination. Dwelling on past mistakes and doing an autopsy on the dead moments of your life only slows you down.

 Reflection Questions:

1. Is there any area of your life where you are spending a lot of time dwelling on the past rather than accepting the present situation and getting going toward achieving your goal(s)?

2. Are there certain areas of your life where you are able to practice the GPS approach more than others?

3. What are the recurring reasons that hold you back from taking action?

4. Is achieving your goals important enough to get you to work on changing your habits, even though it may be uncomfortable?

5. What would you do differently if you had more Forrest Gump qualities?

Recommended Follow-up Action:

1. Take any area of your results, or your life, where you want to accelerate your progress, and ask yourself the following questions:

   i. What outcome am I committed to creating?

   ii. What is the most impactful step I could take next in creating that outcome? In other words, "What's Important Now" (or W.I.N. for short)?

2. Make a list of the top 2 to 3 reasons why you are not in action toward achieving your goal now, and make a commitment to either do something to influence them or accept them as immovable obstacles and work around them.

3. Recognize that regrets, condemnation, and worry will show up. Go back to the above two questions when you find yourself dwelling on regret and worry, and get in action on W.I.N.

There is No "I Can't!" Only "I Don't Want To!"

"If you think you can do a thing or can't do a thing, you are correct."
- Henry Ford

When I look back on all the coaching I have done over the years, it is clear to me that if I had a dollar for every time somebody told me they couldn't do something that they simply didn't want to do, I would be a lot richer than I am today. On countless occasions, I have heard people complain about something somebody was doing that made their job harder, and when asked about whether they had given the person any feedback, they'd say, "I can't possibly do that!" I'd ask, "Well, why can't you?" and their reply would go something like, "Because they can't handle feedback" or, "Because it would ruin our relationship." I have counseled people who hated their jobs, but tolerated them for years, because they "couldn't" quit. When I inquired about the reason, they would state that they couldn't afford the pay cut, or that they didn't know how to go about finding another job.

I want you to consider that we use the phrase, "I can't," very loosely, and while sometimes it is true that we just can't physically do something, like have dinner on the moon in a couple of hours, or kiss our elbow without surgically altering our bodies, most of the time when we say, "I can't," we mean, "I don't want to." For instance, when we say, "I can't quit my job," we mean, "I don't want to quit my job because I am afraid that I may not find another job, or that I may need to take a pay cut." I don't mean to make light of the serious reasons why we may not want to take certain actions. In the case of this example, one's desire to provide for his/her family is certainly a good enough reason to pause and examine the available options before just quitting a job or taking some drastic action that may result in loss of income. However, I am a firm believer that our language makes a profound difference in the context we create in our lives, and the actions we take based on that context. That is why I think it is very important that from this point forward, you be straight about why you are not in action. To that end, rather than saying, "I can't," say, "I don't want to, because ..." (unless of course you are referring to an action that is truly impossible).

The power of taking this approach is that when I say "I can't" do something, the image that it conjures up is that of some force outside of myself preventing me from moving forward and of being overpowered and left with no choice. On the other hand, when I accept having made the choice to not take action and I articulate the reason for doing so, I acknowledge the relevant considerations, and either take responsibility for having made a choice to accept the current situation, or I get in action to change it.

I realize that when emotions are involved, this thought process doesn't seem as black and white as it is here, and it is hard to objectively sort through things you *can't do* versus things you *don't want to do*. As such, I'd encourage you to solicit the help of a coach, friend, or colleague as you go through the process of adopting this language. In my coaching experience, I have found that it is important that I validate and honor the emotions involved *and*, as quickly as possible, get the client to realize that they do have choices, and that they need to take responsibility for their choices. In most cases, there is resistance to accepting that responsibility at first, but I am always thrilled to see the liberation clients feel when they truly grasp this concept and put it into practice.

The advantage of taking this approach is that it transforms your image of who you are, from being a victim, to being a person who is facing challenges and still gets to make choices. The benefit of working with a coach is that you get to articulate what is floating around in your head regarding potential consequences, and distinguish the facts from the fiction that is based purely on your very creative imagination. For instance, when you say, "I don't want to disagree with my boss because I don't want to get fired," it is important to realize that getting fired is probably not a natural consequence of disagreeing with the boss. The natural consequence of a crystal vase dropping on a concrete floor is that it will break into pieces; it will happen every time. Getting fired for voicing your opinion could happen, but it may not.

The other benefit of taking this approach for a test drive is that you get to take an objective view of the pain associated with accepting the current situation versus the pain of taking action to change it. In some cases, you may find that it is far less painful to just accept the current situation than to risk trying to change it and potentially experience other side effects. Yet in other cases, once you have sorted out the real and imaginary consequences of taking action, you may see that taking action to change your circumstances is a far better option. In either case, you will be left liberated by the choice to pursue the path that you believe is the best option.

The Bottom Line:

We often use the language and mindset of "I can't" when we choose not to take the steps that we know we should take. This perpetuates the idea that something outside of us is keeping us from taking that action. Being straight about why we don't want to take those steps puts us back in charge. It puts us back in touch with our power to move forward, or allows us to freely declare that achieving our goal is not worth accepting the consequences of the action it takes to make it happen.

Reflection Questions:

1. Are there certain areas of your work or life in which you have been stagnant and can't seem to break through to the next level of performance?

2. Do you have recurring conversations with yourself about the things you would do if only you could?

3. What are those things that you know would make a difference? Why "can't" you act on them?

4. Are you willing to accept responsibility for those things that you can do, but have chosen not to?

Recommended Follow-up Action:

1. Pick one result, or area of your life, that you would like to make breakthrough progress in.

2. Make a wish list of everything you would change if you had a magic wand. Include everything that comes to mind, whether you have control over it or not.

3. Narrow the list down to a few items that would make the biggest difference in accomplishing what you want.

4. Divide the list into items that you can change and items you "can't."

5. Take every item that you have categorized as something you "can't" do and state it as: "I don't want to, because …" Enlisting the help of a coach would be very beneficial in completing this exercise, as it is not easy to be objective on your own.

6. Make a choice about whether you are going to accept each issue as an immovable obstacle and work with it, or take action to address it.

7. Make a commitment on 1 to 2 actions you are willing to take on in the next week, put them on your schedule, and get them completed.

LESSON 6

Practice Chick-Fil-A® Lemonade Style of Leadership

"No goal is too high if we climb with care and confidence."
- S. Truett Cathy

When I was in college, I worked two jobs just to make ends meet. Eating out was a luxury, and eating at a place that wasn't a fast food joint was definitely a treat that was reserved for very special occasions. Of all the fast food places, my favorite was Chick-Fil-A®. Since those days, I have come to learn more about the company, its founder, the late S. Truett Cathy, and his focus on Servant Leadership.

All I knew back then was that they served a mean chicken sandwich and the best lemonade I had ever had. I mean, this was some serious lemonade. It had some real lemon pulp floating around in it and a taste that was so rich that "it made me wanna slap my mama," as we say in the South! The icing on the cake was that their lemonade was so rich, I could buy one lemonade, pour half of it in another cup, and fill both cups with water and still have two glasses of great lemonade for me and my then girlfriend, to whom I have now been married for over 30 years.

Now, every lemonade connoisseur knows the key to having a rich tasting lemonade is to have lots of lemon juice and lots of sugar. If you have a lot of lemon juice and just a little sugar, the lemonade is too tart, and if it's made the other way around, it's too sweet. If you use a little sugar and a little lemon, it may be balanced, but it gets watered down and doesn't taste like much. By now you might be wondering what lemonade has to do with Transformative Leadership. So allow me to explain.

Let's think of high standards, expectations, and the courage to talk straight and give constructive feedback as lemon juice. Caring for the employees, giving

> *"Transformative Leaders understand and practice Servant Leadership."*

them genuine praise for their accomplishments, understanding their needs and fulfilling those needs would be the sugar. As with any great tasting lemonade, Transformative Leadership also involves a generous amount of both ingredients. Transformative Leaders must have the *courage* to set high standards and expect the best performance out of their employees, and the *consideration* to go about it in a way that consistently empowers and enables the employee. Too much courage and not enough consideration, and you have a boss who stretches people to strive for more, but is feared and unable to cause the employees to grow and deliver superior results. Too much consideration and not enough courage, and you have a harmonious environment where everyone feels comfortable, but there is no real motivation to act, or drive for improvement. Neither of these scenarios results in sustainable growth and excellence.

The other unproductive approach is that of a boss who is not great at positive reinforcement and empowerment, deliberately compromising his high standards. He hesitates to hold people to standards of excellence because he doesn't have enough credibility with them or chips in the bank, so to speak. This results in the equivalent of watered down lemonade. The taste is well balanced, but at a level that offers no satisfaction.

Transformative Leaders understand and practice Servant Leadership. They set high expectations, don't settle for their people being less than extraordinary, and create the balance on the other side of the equation by going out of their way to provide positive reinforcement. They seek to understand the needs of their team members and ensure that they are getting all the support they need to be successful.

So, the next time you enjoy a refreshing glass of rich lemonade, reflect on whether your leadership style has the right balance of lemon and sugar, or if you are lacking one or the other, or both.

. . . .

The Bottom Line:

Leadership is a balancing act on so many fronts. Having the courage to hold people to high standards, and the consideration to do it in a caring manner is paramount. Having the tenacity to lead, and the humility to serve are the key ingredients of Transformative Leadership.

 ### Reflection Questions:

1. Are you exhibiting the right balance of courage and consideration toward your team members?

2. Do your team members know that you deeply care about them as individuals, and that you consider serving them, encouraging them, and setting them up for success to be an important part of your role?

3. Can your team count on you to make the tough calls and hold them to high standards?

4. What specific opportunities do you see to demonstrate more courage or more caring?

Recommended Follow-up Action:

1. Make a list of the tough calls you have made in the past month, and instances where you have held your people to high standards.

2. Make a list of caring gestures you have extended toward your people in the last month. This could include recognizing their accomplishments, doing something to understand their issues and helping to alleviate them.

3. Compare your lists and look for balance. Was one list easier to make than the other? Does one list have more items on it than the other?

4. Now make a list of 2 to 3 actions you can take in the next week to demonstrate your courage, and 2 to 3 actions you can take to demonstrate your caring.

5. Commit to continuously check your approach, and make the necessary adjustments on either side of the equation to make sure you are practicing true Servant Leadership by leading your people courageously, and serving them genuinely.

LESSON 7

Do You Meet 100% of Your Commitments?

"Anything less than a conscious commitment to the important is an unconscious commitment to the unimportant."
- Stephen R. Covey

What percentage of your commitments would you say you meet in life? Fifty? Seventy-five? What if I told you that I meet 100% of my commitments, all the time? Let me explain how I can do it with a little anecdote.

One day, few years ago, my wife of 33 years, who for most of our married life has chosen to be a stay-at-home mom and wife, turned to me and said, "You know, I appreciate that you work and make money to support our family, but you don't do anything around the house. Can you do something to help me out?" Being eager to make my wife happy, I proceeded to ask her what I could do to help, only to find out that she wasn't going to tell me. You guessed it, she wanted *me* to figure it out. So we quibbled back and forth for some time until she realized I wasn't going to get it. She had mercy on me and asked me to wash the dishes and clean the kitchen every night after dinner. I was a happy camper because following orders and cleaning the kitchen wasn't half as painful as trying to figure out what I was supposed to do!

So I got busy, and for weeks I was doing what I needed to do and all was well. Then, one night we had some friends over and they left late. I had to go to work early the next day, so I just sneaked off to bed and didn't clean the kitchen. The next day, I came home and the kitchen had been cleaned and nothing was said. I was grateful for that. I got back on track and did great for another week, and then missed a couple of more nights. To make a long story longer, after a few weeks, I completely fell off the wagon. Here is the interesting thing: Even when I was no longer doing what I had said I would do, I was still meeting my commitment! Do you know how? Because my true commitment was to be lazy, regardless of what I said I was committed to.

I'd like you to consider that you also meet 100% of your commitments, all the time. If you can think of some instances where you are not meeting your commitments, look a little deeper for what your real commitments are. If you have said you were going to get up in the morning and exercise, yet you have been wearing your snooze button out, could it be because you are more committed to sleeping in than you are to the results you would get if you got up and worked out? Of course it is. You are committed to experiencing the immediate pleasure of sleeping in, much more than you are committed to realizing the longer term benefits of having a healthy body. You are indeed meeting your true commitment!

The problem is that most of us are not straight with ourselves and others about what we are really committed to. We say we are committed to something, we come up with all kinds of reasons for not having met that commitment, and after a while we believe our excuses to be completely legitimate reasons to let ourselves off the hook. We say we are 100% committed when in fact, our commitment is very much dependent on other conditions being met. Perhaps we get to the point where we feel like we have done "our part" and now something else has to give before we are willing to put forth more effort.

However, I'll bet you can think of instances where you were 100% committed to something and didn't let anything get in your way. A good example of this is when parents are trying to help their kids learn to walk. I remember picking up my kids dozens of times and always worrying that they would fall back down and hit their heads. One hundred percent commitment in this case means that you pick up the kid 10, 20, 50, or 100 times if you need to until they learn to walk. What if parents weren't 100% committed and there was a limit to how much they would do to help their children learn to walk before they gave up? What if some parents gave up after picking up their kid a few times and said, "I guess this one is going to be a crawler!" Thank goodness we don't see that happening. Can you imagine a bunch of adults crawling around because their parents gave up on them?!

Did you know that when a plane takes off and heads out to a certain destination, 99% of the time, if you drew a line through the middle of the plane and extended it out, it wouldn't go through that destination? Yet the plane ends up landing where it is supposed to go. Why? Because the pilot, or in some cases the auto-pilot, keeps making course corrections until the plane lands at the right airport. What if you and your family were on a plane on your way to a dream vacation in Hawaii, and after a few hours the pilot came out and announced that the plane was going to go to Detroit instead? What if he went on to explain that he was just tired of changing course and was just going to let the plane go wherever it went?

I know that is pretty extreme and it doesn't happen very often, if at all, but it happens all too frequently in our lives. We set our sights on a goal and we give it a try, and we even hang in there through some trouble and continue to make those course corrections. But, at some point, just when we think we have done our part or we have done enough, we throw our hands up and say, "I guess we are going to Detroit!" Worse yet, we don't acknowledge that we are no longer committed to making it to Hawaii, so instead we blame the winds, storms, the plane, and all kinds of other things for having gotten us off course.

The truth is that you cannot be partially committed any more than a woman can be a little pregnant. You are either committed or not. It is honorable to declare that you are no longer committed to something and accept the consequences. But, an unfulfilled commitment is still a commitment, and as long as you remain committed, there is always something to do to fulfill the commitment.

The Bottom Line:

We always win whatever game we want to play. We spend our time and money, and deploy our resources toward exactly what we are committed to, but sometimes we are not straight about what our real commitment is.

Reflection Questions:

1. Are there commitments that you have made that you have not followed through on?

2. Are there results you want to produce, and relationships you want to improve, that you have said you are 100% committed to, but you now realize that you have been conditionally committed to?

3. What external factors have you been blaming for your lack of progress?

4. What is holding you back internally? What are you committed to more that is holding you back from achieving the results you say you are committed to?

 Recommended Follow-up Action:

1. Pick one result that you are committed to delivering.

2. List all the reasons you have had for not being in action to deliver this result.

3. Make a choice to declare yourself 100% committed, and get in action to do what needs to be done, or to let the stakeholders know that you are not committed to delivering that result, and take what you get.

4. Accept the positive and negative consequences of your choice and stop complaining about the consequences you don't like.

LESSON 8

You Have the Right to be Miserable!
... But Why Would You Want to Be?

"The destination isn't in finding yourself. The destination is in the search."
- Thomas Warfield

A group of friends were taking an overnight ride on a train that was equipped with a fully stocked bar, great music and a dance floor, and they were having a great time. Eventually, one of them noticed that one of their friends was just sitting in the corner, deep in thought. He approached him and asked why he wasn't joining the festivities. The poor, sad fellow proceeded to tell his friend that he owed some guys $5,000, and that they were going to be waiting for him when he got off the train the next day to beat him up if he didn't pay them back. The friend immediately offered to pay the guy's debt and assured him that all was going to be well. Once the shock and disbelief wore off, the sad fellow got up, thanked his friend, and joined the party. They had a great time, and when they arrived at their destination, the guy who owed the money went up to his friend to collect the money to pay off his debt. As he was thanking his friend profusely for this huge favor, he was informed by his friend that he didn't actually have the money. In deep fear and anguish, the guy asked, "Why did you say you were going to pay them off if you didn't have the money?" to which the friend responded, "I knew you were going to get beat up, so I figured you might as well have a good time on the way!"

You can imagine what might have been going through the guy's mind, right? I'm thinking he felt betrayed. He was probably thinking, "I could have been miserable the whole time and you ruined it for me!" I can't tell you how many times I have come across people who have absolutely refused to believe in a brighter future just because they were afraid of getting excited about a positive outcome that may not have come to fruition. It is like if the guy in the story said, "No thanks, I don't want you to pay those guys because you may be pulling my leg, and if I am going to get beat up anyway, I'd rather just be miserable the whole way!" Maybe it doesn't play out exactly like that for us. We don't say it out loud, but we quietly refuse to go for something big for the fear that we may not achieve it.

My question to you is: Why not declare a huge success in achieving something that you are committed to in your life even if there is a possibility that you might fall short? What have you got to lose? First of all, life is a lot more fun when you have hope in a brighter future. Secondly, most of the time when you believe in something good happening, you begin to see opportunities to bring it about. So, while we absolutely have the right to be miserable, why do we insist on exercising that right? Why is it that when someone is very positive about something, we tend to try to discredit them and drag them down, as opposed to joining in on their optimism and acting like it is all going to be alright?

As a leader, the consequences of this choice are even more profound because, ideally, it is the leader who ought to be the instigator of optimism and belief in a brighter future in the organization. We live in a culture that promotes "under-promising and over-delivering." That may be prudent when you are making commitments to Wall Street, and you know that your stock price would take a beating if you didn't deliver what you promised. However, this mentality has gone too far and has robbed the majority of people and organizations of the joy of declaring something bold, rising to the occasion of delivering it, and feeling the satisfaction that would compel them to keep stretching themselves.

The Bottom Line:

We often shy away from setting stretch targets for the fear that we may not achieve them. We have nothing to lose and everything to gain by envisioning a transformative future because, at best, we will achieve it, and at worst, we will have transformed the quality of our journey in pursuit of a transformation we are committed to.

Reflection Questions:

1. Are there hopes and dreams that you had that you chose to let go of because you didn't want to be disappointed again?

2. Have you ever treated the positive people in your life as if they were naïve, and tried to convince them that their "pie-in-the-sky" ideas were not going to materialize?

3. What future can you envision that would energize you? Are you willing to begin to live your life as if that future has real possibilities and quit worrying about it not coming true?

Recommended Follow-up Action:

1. Pick one result, one relationship, or one aspect of your life that is important to you and write down what the ideal state would look like. Describe how you would feel, what you would see, and so on, when you got there.

2. Begin to tell other people around you about that future you envisioned, and describe it to them such that they believe it and get excited about it too.

3. When the worries show up about that future not coming to pass, either trace them down to actions you are going to take, and take them, or set them aside as if to assume that your friend is going to take care of it.

LESSON 9

Do Unto Others
As They Would like to be Done Unto Them!

"You never really understand a person until you consider things from his point of view – until you climb into his skin and walk around in it."
- Harper Lee

I don't know about other husbands out there, but I can admit that my wife has always been much more proactive than me in seeking out ways to improve our marriage and our parenting skills, among other things. It took me years to finally get on board with that sort of thing, but I'm so glad I did. One of the activities we did together was attend a marriage maintenance course, which was intended for couples who had a good marriage already, but were interested in taking it to the next level.

We both learned some very valuable lessons in that class, many of which were quite counter-intuitive and extremely useful. One of the many lessons we learned was that we both tend to treat the other person as we want to be treated. You might wonder what is wrong with that approach. After all, the Golden Rule says, "Do unto others as you would like them to do unto you." Right? Given my reverence and respect for the source, I am in no position to question the validity of that rule, and I know that in so many aspects of our lives, the Golden Rule is an invaluable guide. However, like any other good thing, you have to know how to use it as it is intended.

Certainly, when it comes to the bottom line and ethical matters where we all have the same preferences, we ought to do unto others as we would like them to do unto us. If I don't want someone to steal from me, it is a good indication that they wouldn't want me to steal from them. But in areas where we have varying preferences, the literal interpretation of the Golden Rule may go against the very essence of it.

For instance, as a frequent traveler, I would really like to buy a pair of noise-canceling headphones to wear on airplanes so I can drown out the white noise, and crying babies, but I don't think my wife would be very happy if I went out and bought her a set of headphones for her birthday, just because I want one. While the Golden Rule is still valid in the sense that, "If you want others to buy you something you want for your birthday, buy them something they want for theirs," going out and doing exactly the same thing that you would want others to do for you does not work very well.

What my wife and I learned was that just because she preferred to have a conversation about her day when I came home, didn't mean I wanted the same thing. She learned that I needed some "cave time" before I was ready to discuss anything, and I learned not to jump into my problem solving mode simply because she wanted to vent and discuss how her day went. In other words, we learned that we ought to do unto the other as he/she would like to be done unto him/her. This lesson has served us well.

Leaders often make the mistake of assuming that everyone wants the same thing done the same way, rather than adjusting their behavior to the culture of the organization, or the person they are working with. Of course, again, at some level we all want the same things, but its delivery is much more effective if it is tailored. For instance, no one prefers to be kept in the dark. Generally speaking, we all would rather be kept informed, but a leader who communicates like a TV set, the same way no matter who is watching, will miss out on the opportunity to get his point across. I certainly learned that lesson during my international assignments in Germany and Thailand. Beyond the obvious language barriers that had to be overcome, the preferred styles of communication couldn't have been more different between the two places. I had to use a communication style that was much more direct and to the point in Germany, and much less so in Thailand, in order to be effective.

Transformative Leaders are intentional when it comes to learning about their audience and the people they are leading and serving. They lead in a way that is effective, rather than sticking to their own ways and expecting everyone else to adapt to them. Even if you are not dealing with different cultures and you lead a seemingly homogeneous group of people, it would be naïve to assume that all people have the same preference in how they communicate. In fact, situations like that are often more perilous as the obvious signs of diversity do not exist to alert us to modify our approach and style, and we are caught off-guard just when we think everything ought to go smoothly.

The Bottom Line:

The assumption that everyone wants to be treated as we want to be treated certainly serves us well in extending basic human courtesy and respect. In our day-to-day interactions, however, we come across many opportunities to tailor our communication style and specific approaches to how others want to be treated, which may differ in some ways from how we want to be treated. Being in tune with the preferences of our team members serves us well.

 ## Reflection Questions:

1. Are there individuals or groups of people in your organization who consistently fail to meet expectations?

2. Are you sure that your communication style is such that it is reaching them?

3. How much do you know about your organization and what motivates different individuals and teams?

4. Do you communicate the same way with everyone, or do you take into account their preferences and modify your style?

 ## Recommended Follow-up Action:

1. Make it your mission to connect with your immediate team members and get to know what motivates them, and what turns them off.

2. Seek and act on feedback on your personal communication style and what you could do to be more effective.

3. Think of a specific message that you consider to be extremely important to the success of your organization and devise a multi-pronged communication approach that will reach the various people in the organization.

What is Your Life Made Up Of?

"I am not what happened to me, I am what I choose to become."
- C.G. Jung

Have you ever thought about what your life is made up of? If I asked you to tell me the components that make up the chair you are sitting in, or any other object around you, you could probably break it down and list the parts that make up that object. Now, if I asked you what your life is made of, even though you may not have specifically thought about it, I'm sure you can think of some things. Most people say things like, "my job, my family, my relationships, my material possessions," and the like. If they decide to go a little deeper, sometimes they refer to their faith, values, health, and so on.

Consider that while all those answers are true to a degree, in that those are things that you have in your life and they influence your life in some form or fashion, they are not what your life is made up of. You can see evidence of this everyday as you come across people who have the best of those things in their lives, but are not satisfied. Then there are others who may not even have a fraction of what one could have, be it a great job, lots of money, great friends, and still consider themselves to have a great life.

I submit that your life is made up of your thoughts, words, actions, and habits, which form your character and ultimately determine your destiny. Circumstances, people, and things influence your life, but you hold the power to alter how you process the impact that those external factors have on you. Whether you take control of your thoughts, words, and so on, or you allow your circumstances to be in control, your perception of how your life has turned out is a sum total of what you think, what you say, what you do, and what habits you develop.

The great news here is that you are not at the mercy of the people, things, and experiences you have had, or currently have in your life. All that you need in order to have a wonderful life is inside you. You just need to be reminded of who you really are and the power you possess to live an extraordinary life.

I have known plenty of people who seemed to have it all by the standards of the world, and yet lived miserable lives. I have also known a few who live in a state of bliss, in spite of there being no apparent reason as to why they should. One particular person who comes to mind is a fellow I met a few years back who found out he had a serious disease and appeared to know that his days were numbered. I don't know the specifics of his prognosis and what caused him to have a profoundly different outlook on life than most people I know. All I know is that he decided to live the rest of his life in service of God through serving the homeless. He sold practically everything he owned, moved into a small room, and dedicated every waking moment of his life to soliciting people for donations of food, and drinks, and time to serve the poor. In this process, not only did he transform countless lives, but he himself was always, even in the worst of conditions, the happiest person I have ever met. He was full of life and constantly ministering to anybody whose path crossed his.

He is gone now, but he left a legacy, not only in how he treated the poor, but also in teaching the rest of us that no matter what your situation, you can control your thoughts, you can choose the words that come out of your mouth, and you can take actions that are in line with what you are committed to and what you set out to achieve. You can determine the quality of your life in spite of your circumstances.

You don't have to know how to control your thoughts to subscribe to this idea. If you accept that it is possible to live a peaceful and powerful life in the face of unfavorable circumstances, you will begin to attract the knowledge and wisdom to live a life of success and significance regardless of your situation. In fact, if you believe it is possible for you to do so, you will find several lessons in the pages of this book that will enable you to take some giant steps in that direction.

As long as you remain committed to the journey, you will begin to see a huge difference in the quality of your life immediately, in spite of the ups and downs. You won't believe the burden that gets lifted off of you in a matter of weeks or even days. I'd suggest you start small with some of your habits, at work or in your personal life. If you have habits that are destructive and do not serve your purpose, commit to cutting them back to occasional actions if you cannot completely eliminate them. If there are actions you are taking that don't serve you or your community, commit to not taking those actions again. If there are words you habitually speak that are negative and are perhaps the source of certain actions, remove those words from your vocabulary. And of course, the most powerful step is to choose your thoughts. As shown in the figure below, the further upstream you go, the more impact you have on your life. If you reduce or eliminate certain habits, that is good, but if you nip it in the bud before it is a thought that you dwell on, and eventually speak and act on, then it is much more powerful.

Change Your Thoughts, Change Your Destiny

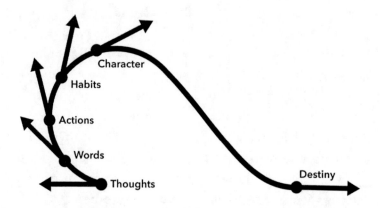

I am a firm believer in the rumble strips they put on the side of highways to alert you when you are about to veer off the road. In fact, I am very clear that those things saved my life, or at least spared me some serious injury, when I nearly fell asleep at the wheel on at least two occasions. The same idea can work in your effort to be intentional about transforming the quality of your life. If you are trying to get rid of certain habits, why not establish clear "rumble strips" that indicate when you are heading off course, and when you hit them, take a predetermined action to keep from going there?

If I am a recovering alcoholic, I might establish my "rumble strip" to be a trip to a bar. When the idea shows up in a conversation, it immediately raises all kinds of red flags and I decide to do something else. I am not going to go to the bar and hope to have enough discipline to not have a drink. I might even establish a safer set of "rumble strips" further upstream. I may stop hanging out with my old drinking buddies. The bottom line is that when you establish warning signs and act on them, you have a much better chance of not acting on the automatic thoughts that don't serve your purpose.

Let me share a couple of tricks with you that will make this process easier and much more practical than the way we normally go about it. We normally try to fight bad thoughts with good thoughts. In other words, we try to think our way into a new way of behaving, but that hardly ever works. The only way to stop your unwanted thoughts is to speak or behave the opposite. First, let's discuss speaking your way into a new way of thinking.

I practice this often as I have two adult kids who are in the midst of transition in their lives, and I often have negative thoughts around how their futures might turn out. In those cases, I just speak, out loud, words of gratitude that I have children who are blessed, prosperous, and successful. I have found that I cannot possibly think something different while I am speaking these words. So, at the very least, my words stop the incessant stream of negative thoughts, and in some cases they replace them with positive thoughts. This is because it is impossible for you to think one thing and speak another. If you need practical proof of this, here is something you can try. Start counting in your head from 1 to 30 and when you get to 10, speak your name and address, and the name of the company where you work out loud while continuing to count in your head. Try it! You can't do it. You cannot keep up with one stream of thought going through your head while you are speaking about something entirely different.

You might be concerned that people may think you're crazy if they see you talking to yourself in a public place. Well, I have a remedy for that too. You can put one of those wireless earpieces in your ear and let everybody think you are on the phone! How about that? Better yet, you could actually speak to someone else who is committed to helping you replace your negative thoughts with positive ones. Engage in dialogue with people who are not only committed to letting you vent, but also to helping you get into a more productive conversation. Next time you are overcome by worry and fear, don't go looking for someone who will sympathize with you. Find someone who is willing to listen as you vent, and is nevertheless committed to help you transform your thinking.

Now, let's talk about behaving your way into a new way of thinking. If you have ever snoozed your clock in the morning when you knew you should have just gotten up, you know what it's like to have that dialogue with yourself and decide to snooze just one more time. Now, what if you tried a different approach? What if you let that conversation go on and while it was still going on, you got up out of bed, turned off your alarm and started your morning routine? You might be saying things in your head that should probably not be mentioned here, but you're behaving according to your commitment, not your immediate emotion. I have tried this with morning workouts—which I am not very fond of—and found out that after a few minutes of actually doing what I had to do to get dressed and get into my workout routine, my thoughts changed. In other words, I behaved my way into a new way of thinking.

One thing to keep in mind is that when I speak of changing your thoughts, I am not talking about the automatic stream of thoughts that go through your mind without your consent. That will always be there and there is not much you can do about it. As the Chinese proverb goes, the trick is not in keeping the birds from flying over your head, but keeping them from building a nest in your hair, so to speak. The thoughts will come and go, but you can have a significant impact on your life if you deliberately shift your thinking when you realize that the automatic thoughts that just showed up are no good for you.

The Bottom Line:

What shapes the quality of our lives is not what we have in our lives, but how we generate and process our experience of life through our thoughts, words, actions and habits. It is these things which ultimately determine our character and significantly influence our destiny. The ability to see this puts the "ball in our court" to determine the quality of our lives, independent of external factors.

Reflection Questions:

1. Are there certain habits that you know you should eliminate? What are they?

2. Are there certain actions you take periodically that you know you need to stop? What are they?

3. Do you speak negative things into your life and the lives of others around you? What is the language you need to eliminate or modify?

4. Can you trace the words, actions, and habits that you don't want in your life to thoughts that you entertain? What are they?

Recommended Follow-up Action:

1. Commit to being open to learning about how to shift the quality of your life (thoughts, words, etc.) even if your circumstances don't change at all. Don't get hung up on knowing how before you commit. The "how" will show up soon enough.

2. Pick a specific aspect of your life that you are not satisfied with, and make a list of all the thoughts, words, actions, and habits that you would eliminate in order to impact that area of your life.

3. Begin the process of adopting new thoughts, words, and actions now!

4. If you fall off the wagon and feel discouraged, just get back on track and keep moving forward.

LESSON 11

Keep the Passion! Ditch the Drama!

"Nothing great in the world has ever been accomplished without passion."
- Georg Wilhelm Friedrich Hegel

In my experience in leading organizations and coaching clients, I have come across countless occurrences of people being so overwhelmed and emotional about a situation that their very behavior was making the problem worse. I have also heard people defend their destructive behavior as a sign of their passion. After all, if they didn't care, they wouldn't get so mad! On the other hand, I believe we have all known people who are so easygoing all the time that you wonder if they ever get excited about anything, and while the positive effect of them being able to remain calm and focused is clear to others, sometimes their level of commitment and passion is brought into question.

I have personally been at both ends of this spectrum on different occasions in my life. There have been times when I was so stressed that, as a matter of survival, I resorted to having a "whatever" attitude, which reduced the stress but put me in a zone where I felt like I wasn't making a difference. By the same token, there have been other times when I was so passionate about a cause that no matter what barriers I ran into, I would press ahead and experience significant frustration with anything and anybody that was perceived to a be a barrier. My experience at both ends of the spectrum has been negative. Sometimes, too much drama, driven by my passion, left me exhausted, and at other times, my attempt to limit my passion to reduce my drama left me indifferent and unfulfilled.

There is a widespread assumption that there is a correlation between how much passion you have for a subject and how much drama you experience around it, either privately or publicly. There is good reason for this assumption because generally the two go hand-in-hand. If you think of a topic that you have no passion for, you'll find it creates very little drama in your life. By contrast, if you pick a topic that you have significant passion for, you'll find that the very source of your passion is also at the root of the corresponding drama it creates.

What if you could get the best of both worlds? What if you could keep the passion and ditch the drama? What if you could experience the exhilaration of being completely passionate about, and fully dedicated to, a certain outcome, but not be fazed by barriers along the way? What if you could remain 100% committed to the cause in the face of setbacks? This is actually quite possible, but it requires an entirely different view of passion and drama than the one that you are, perhaps, used to.

Consider that passion and drama are completely independent of one another and they can be dialed up and down independently. In fact, they are such polar opposites that they cannot coexist in the same space. If this seems completely counter to the common view we discussed earlier, it's because it is. While it is true that certain topics spark passion and drama in our lives while others do not, it is important to consider that, at any given point in time, we can only operate in one realm or the other, never both. In other words, the second you enter the world of overwhelm and drama, you have left the realm of passion for the outcome you say you are committed to. And, the minute you truly embody your passion and commitment, you act in the face of undesirable circumstances with no drama at all.

The source of passion is the commitment to a certain outcome and an intense desire to experience, or cause others to experience, the benefits of that outcome. On the other hand, the source of drama is fear and worry. Passion is about expressing your commitment in the present moment. Drama is about letting your regrets about past events, or worries about a possible future, cause you to take your eye off the ball and lose sight of what's important right now. Passion is personal and it can exist independent of others. Drama needs an audience and without one, it dies down quickly. Just like toddlers can fall down and get right back up and move on if there is no one there, but often cry and scream if their parent is around, adults also feed off of their audience and intensify their drama accordingly. When you are truly committed to an outcome, there is only passion. When you pretend to be committed, there is a whole lot of drama.

The following shows a few attitudes and behaviors that distinguish passion from drama:

PASSION	DRAMA
Proactive; Actions based on the outcome you are committed to	Reactive; Actions based on what has happened or what is happening now
Innovation	Frustration
Abundance mentality	Scarcity mentality
Faith in a positive outcome	Fear of a negative outcome

PASSION	DRAMA
"I am the one!"	"Someone else needs to make it happen!"
"It's not about me!"	"It's all about me!"
"What's the most important step I can take next?"	"Who can I blame for the situation we are in?"
Intentional; Hard	Automatic; Easy
Energizing; Rewarding	Painful; Draining

Passion Versus Drama

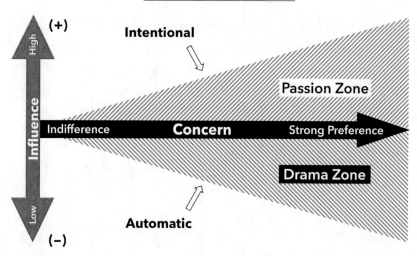

Of course, it is one thing to understand and accept this reasoning, but it is another to be able to manage your emotions such that you keep yourself in the passion zone and out of the drama zone. That's why it is not enough to intellectually subscribe to the concept. If you are committed to progressively reducing the amount of drama you experience in life, you must examine where and how drama usually shows up in your life, what triggers it, how it can be prevented, and what to do when, in spite of your best efforts, it shows up anyway. Let's look at some of these next.

There are a number of reasons for drama to show up. It could be because:

- We and others perceive drama as validation of the extent of our passion.

- It is easier and more fun, painful as it may be, than acting on our passion and being proactive.

- We focus more on our regrets about the past and worries about the future than the opportunities of the present moment.

- We predict the worst case scenario, look for and find evidence for it, and act accordingly.

- We focus more on the problem (what we don't want), rather than the possibility (what we do want).

- We pretend to be 100% committed when we are not.

Your reasons and triggers for your personal brand of drama may be entirely different than what is listed above. If that's the case, disregard these and focus on your insights into what resonates with you.

Once you have identified why and how drama shows up, it is important to be strategic about how to prevent it. The best way I know to tackle your drama is to let it disappear in the face of a bigger commitment. Supercharge your commitment by setting goals that are not about you. Tie your goals to a greater purpose, and envision the greater purpose having been fulfilled already.

Once you are hooked on the vision of a commitment bigger than yourself having been fulfilled, it is hard to stay in the drama zone, even if you go there for a few minutes. You're going to want to get back in action to cause your reality to match the vision that you are already hooked on. Likewise, the other thing that helps prevent drama is to declare your intentions to others and ask them to be your accountability partners. This makes it much more compelling to live into the future that you have declared, and you will receive those much-needed nudges when you feel like giving up. The added bonus is that you will energize others to join the cause.

So, what happens if you do all of that and drama still sneaks up on you? The first thing to do is take responsibility! I'd suggest that you refrain from talking or acting on whatever emotions you are feeling at that moment until you have had some time to consider the situation. I'd also suggest you genuinely seek honest feedback from a reliable accountability partner. Most importantly, after you have given your emotions some time to subside, ask yourself, "What outcome am I committed to?" and, "What is the most important thing I can do to make it happen?" Then act on the answers. If you have allowed your drama to cause you to behave in a manner that is counter to your true commitment, publicly admit that you have not been behaving based on your commitment and declare your intentions to make specific course corrections.

These are all general suggestions, and although some of them may resonate with you, their true purpose is to spark some insight in you about your unique brand of drama and what will work best for you, personally.

The Bottom Line:

Passion and drama stem from the same source, which is our strong desire for a certain result or outcome. When we care deeply about something, we also tend to experience drama in that area of our life, but if we don't care, there is no passion or drama. Therefore, we have falsely concluded that passion and drama go hand-in-hand when, in fact, they are two mutually exclusive realms. Understanding this distinction helps us be intentional about expressing our passion without suffering the drama that we have associated with it.

Reflection Questions:

1. Do you experience some recurring drama in any aspect of your personal or professional life? If so, what is it?

2. What are the common triggers of drama in your life?

3. What steps can you take to prevent the most prevalent drama in your life?

4. Are you willing to entertain the possibility that you can keep the passion but ditch the drama? What would happen to your quality of life and effectiveness if that were to happen?

Recommended Follow-up Action:

1. Identify one recurring drama that you are willing to work on eliminating.

2. Study what you have identified, and examine the triggers, how they can be prevented, and what you can do to diffuse them when they show up.

3. Make a commitment to actions you are going to take based on your answers to question 2.

4. Find an accountability partner and share your plan of action with him/her, and ask your partner for honest feedback on how you are doing along the way.

5. Observe yourself in action and keep making course corrections, no matter how many times you fail to follow through.

6. Examine the magnitude of the specific drama you are working on again in three weeks, and acknowledge the progress you have made and/or make further course corrections

LESSON 12

Leadership Starts with "Be-There-ship"

"The first responsibility of a leader is to define reality. The last is to say thank you. In between, the leader is a servant." - Max DePree

The Transformative Leader recognizes the critical role of what I call "Be-There-ship." There are four dimensions to Be-There-ship, which will be explained in this lesson:

1 - Be Physically Present:

Early in my career, I worked at a manufacturing plant with about 1,600 employees. I remember the days when I was a few minutes late and I had to make the dreaded long walk from the guard shack to the entrance of the building. You see, the entire walkway was in plain sight of the plant manager who had a nice, large corner office with a glass wall overlooking the manicured lawn in front of the plant.

The plant manager was the highest-ranking person there, so high on the food chain that I couldn't even begin to imagine what it would be like to ever have his job. I had met him on a few occasions and we had had a few conversations, but not enough to subdue the butterflies in my stomach every time I ran into him in the cafeteria or the hallway.

One day, I noticed that he had moved into an office that already had three other people in it, a few doors down from my office. He had just camped out at a vacant desk and was working out of that office. I was perplexed. I didn't understand why he would do something like that. Was he spying? Did he get demoted? How were we supposed to act around him? I'm sure a lot of us were trying to figure out what was going on, but after a couple of weeks or so, things began to feel normal again. We still weren't sure what his office move was all about, but he was able to interact with people in the office, and on the production floor adjacent to the office, much more effectively without all the formalities of a "leadership visit."

This was years before I learned about what the Japanese call *gemba*, which refers to being where the action takes place and closing the gap between leadership and the rest of the organization. Since then, I have randomly moved my office closer to the action multiple times, even if it meant I had to work out of a small and noisy space. As a plant manager, I even had a simple portable desk on wheels made for a couple of hundred bucks that I would move around to different parts of the plant so I could be on the production floor as I was working on my computer.

Even if you don't physically move your office, being around people in their workplace, visiting them, and being present in their space is much appreciated once you get past the initial "what is he/she doing here?" stage. What I have also found is that leaders who earn their people's respect and establish credibility with their organization generate enthusiasm and increase productivity when they walk into a room. So, being present to provide positive feedback, or actively demonstrating the desire to understand the real problems people are dealing with, goes a long way.

This approach is portrayed very well in one of my favorite TV shows, *Undercover Boss*, in which the CEO of a company goes to various locations within the company and works with front-line people under the guise of being a newly hired employee. In disguise, the CEOs are afforded the opportunity to experience the reality of what their people are working with. This not only gives the boss the opportunity to remove barriers that are getting in the way of productivity, but once the boss reveals his/her true identity, it turns out to be a great morale booster for the front-line employees to see that the boss is willing to work alongside them.

You don't have to be a CEO or be on a TV show to actively be present and demonstrate your genuine desire to see the world through the eyes of those who count on you to lead them. A small attempt to understand their world goes a long way.

2 - Be Available:

Make sure that your people know you are available to them, and that they know how to reach you if they need to. It is important for them to be self-directed, and to know that you don't want to rescue them every time they get into a situation that could bring them some growth and development; however, it is equally important for them to know that if they need you when you are not physically present, they have license to reach out to you and that you will get back to them at your earliest convenience.

Leaders sometimes hesitate to make themselves *too* accessible because they don't want people to disregard the chain of command. My experience is that 95% of people will use good judgment on when they should contact you and when they should find alternate means of resolving their issue. The icing on the cake is that you will have a direct opportunity to coach and calibrate the others who come to you with issues they can either resolve themselves or bring to someone else's attention.

3 - Be in Their World:

Have you ever been in a conversation with someone who is in their own world and not aware that you are even there? They are having a monologue directed at you but their attention is every bit on themselves and certainly not you. I have come across a few people like that. These are people who communicate like a TV set. They don't care who is watching. They have something to say and they say it without any regard to your reactions, questions, or body language.

The ability to practice this leadership attribute goes beyond the techniques and skills of listening and interacting. It has to do with genuinely valuing people enough to be interested in their triumphs and challenges. It is not about sympathy, but empathy. It is not so much about the quantity of contact, but the quality of every interface.

When Transformative Leaders are in a conversation with someone, they are *there* in the other person's world, listening to them and understanding their reality. They are in tune with body language so they can truly understand the other person's state of mind and emotions. This not only leaves the other person with an experience of having been valued and understood, it also ensures that the message the leader intends to get across actually lands "over there," as intended.

4 - Be There for Them:

Transformative Leaders are there for their people. They can be counted on to serve their people in whatever capacity is needed at the time. Sometimes, this may involve listening, offering a suggestion, or committing to a certain action. Most of us have had bosses we knew we couldn't count on to be there for us. Some of us have been fortunate enough to have had bosses who were there and really cared about us as individuals; they were there for us when we needed them for professional or personal support.

I can honestly say that there are more than a few moments in my nearly 30-year professional life that stand out to me as proof that I was doing something right as a leader, and they had nothing to do with work. I was the first person that one of my employees called when he and his wife, who also worked in my plant, found out that their son had passed away. Many years before that, one of my employees called me in the middle of the night when he and his wife experienced a traumatic situation in their lives, so that I could be with them at the hospital. I don't bring these up to boast about my leadership abilities, but to say that when something like that happens and you can see that what you have invested in a relationship has paid off in the form of trust and respect, there is no breaking that bond. No circumstance is going to come between you and the other person, as you have proven yourself to be worthy of their loyalty. Of course, this has to be done out of your genuine care and concern for people, not as a strategy to get something out of them.

The more aspects of "Be-There-ship" you can master and consistently demonstrate to your team, the more you will see that they will reciprocate the same sentiment. That two-way street of being there creates magic in your culture and your results.

The Bottom Line:

*Leadership is about **being there** for those who are counting on you to lead them. Being there can be demonstrated in a variety of* *ways, the culmination of which creates a solid foundation on which Transformative Leaders build engagement and loyalty.*

 ## Reflection Questions:

1. How much time do you spend on the front line where most of the value of your products and services is generated?

2. Do you make sure that people beyond your direct-reports or your administrative assistant can easily reach you?

3. Do you pay attention to people's reactions and body language, and do you pause to let them engage in the dialogue and interact when you are communicating with them?

4. Can you think of experiences and signs that tell you your people can count on you and that they don't hesitate to come to you when they need something, personally or professionally?

 ## Recommended Follow-up Action:

1. Assess yourself against the dimensions of "Be-There-ship," and identify what you are doing well and where you need to do better.

2. Be intentional about identifying behaviors that you are going to begin exhibiting.

3. Publicly declare your assessment and intentions, ask for feedback, and request people to hold you to your declarations. If you are not yet ready to do this with a large audience, start with a few people or even one person and build from there.

Expect Compliance, Inspire Commitment

"Level 5 leaders look in the mirror, not out the window, to apportion responsibility for poor results, never blaming other people, external factors, or bad luck." - *Jim Collins*

Over the years, I have heard many bosses complain about their employees having an entitlement mentality. I have to admit that I have felt that way about some people in my organizations from time to time. You just can't do enough for those people. They feel like just because you are the boss, you owe them everything, and often nothing you do seems to be good enough. They take their paycheck for granted and don't want to do anything beyond the minimum.

One of the greatest epiphanies I ever had as a leader was that *I* was the one with the entitlement mentality. I felt like if my people didn't give their best, they were cheating me out of something I was entitled to. On numerous occasions, privately and sometimes publicly, I would blame them and shift all the responsibility for poor results to them rather than myself.

The truth is that your people don't owe you their full commitment. All they owe you is compliance. You give them a paycheck and you ought to expect them to fulfill the responsibilities that have been laid out as part of their job. If you want their commitment, you need to earn it. Their commitment is certainly worth a lot more to you and your business than their compliance, but you can't buy it. The only way you get their commitment is by creating an environment in which they offer it up for free.

The best evidence of this is the millions of hours every year that people all around the world spend doing volunteer work toward a cause they feel committed to. I'm sure you can think of something that you are committed to that you would do for free. When people get a sense that what they are doing is worthwhile and their personal contribution matters, they go above and beyond the call of duty to make sure it is done right. I assure you that some of the people on your team who are struggling to barely fulfill their basic responsibilities are involved in important activities in their lives outside of work. They may be coaching their kid's team, or volunteering at their place of worship, or performing important services in the community. They have it in them to do the same at work, but for some reason their inclination to do so at work is being hindered.

I have been blessed in my career to have worked with so many people whose dedication and tireless efforts far exceeded my expectations. I couldn't afford to pay them for what they brought to the party because their contribution was simply priceless. In every case, these people were motivated by something other than their paycheck or benefits.

As illustrated in the figure below, to increase the level of participation, and to take people from indifference to compliance, you must remove the "dissatisfiers." For example, if paychecks are not ready when they are expected to be, people will be dissatisfied. Making sure paychecks are issued on time is removing a dissatisfier, but it is not necessarily a motivator. In other words, people don't get up in the morning and say, "Wow,

I am going to get a paycheck this week, so let me get out there and give it my all!" If they get their paycheck on time, they are simply not dissatisfied, which always helps.

Accountability Versus Entitlement

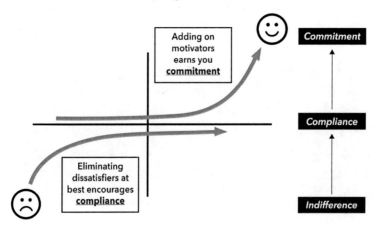

Now, in order to go beyond compliance and earn commitment, you must add in "motivators," which almost never have anything to do with extrinsic rewards such as pay or other tangibles. People are always motivated more by intrinsic rewards, which come in a lot of different forms. For some people, it may be a genuine expression of your appreciation. For someone else, it may be the opportunity to chat with you over a cup of coffee. For yet another person, it may be the opportunity to learn additional skills so they can continue to expand their impact and influence. Extrinsic rewards, such as pay and benefits and formal recognition, must be administered consistently and uniformly, or else they become a source of dissatisfaction; but I have learned that when it comes to intrinsic rewards, the more personalized and the more random they are, the more they are appreciated.

Predictable and consistent recognition that assumes everyone is motivated by the same thing generally doesn't do the trick. When you get to know people and ensure that they receive the type of recognition that they personally appreciate, you are more likely to earn their commitment.

Now, let's talk about the notion that money does not motivate people, because I can just imagine what some of you must be thinking by now. I have had the very conversation you would like to have with me about money being a motivator many, many times in my workshops. First, let me admit that even I have, at times, had the illusion of having been motivated by money. I am generally very motivated when I receive an above-average pay raise. I break the news to my wife and we go out and celebrate, but over the years, it has become crystal clear to me that it is not the extra money I will be making that creates those emotions of pride and joy. It is *what I make it mean* about myself and just how much I am valued that is the source of how I feel.

I am confident that this is the case for you as well. Before you reject the idea, allow me to demonstrate. Imagine that you are sitting in a meeting with a group of your peers, and your boss walks into the room. He hands everyone an envelope and says, "I just wanted to let you guys know how much I appreciate what you do, and I'd like to give you a small token of my appreciation." You look around the room and sense everyone's anticipation of what might be in the envelope. The boss leaves the room and everyone rushes to open their envelope and shortly thereafter, high-fives are flying around. You open your envelope and there is a check written to you for $10K! How do you feel? I'm guessing pretty happy and appreciated.

Now, imagine that as you start talking to other people and as you share in the festivities, you find out that everybody else in the room only got $5K and you appear to be the only person who got $10K. How do you feel now? I'm guessing you are feeling even better about your check because not only you are $10K richer, you are also assured that you are valued more than everyone else.

Now, let's imagine a different scenario. What if you found out everybody else got $25K and you were the only one who got $10K? How are you feeling now? Of course, when I ask this question in my workshops, somebody is bound to say, "I still feel pretty good because I have $10K that I didn't have before," but we all know that is not entirely true. If you're straight with yourself, you'll admit that you are feeling pretty deflated, even though you have more money in your pocket, that money now carries a message that says, "I am not very valued around here compared to my peers."

In all three scenarios that I described, you have $10K more than you did before. In one case you are happy, in another case you are totally elated, and in yet another, you are ticked off and disappointed. So, is it really the money, or is it what you make it mean, that motivates or demotivates you? Sure, most of us would like to have more money and more benefits, but let's face it, most of the time the pay raises that we get will not significantly shift our lifestyle, and even if they do, we quickly get used to it and set our sights on the next level of spending we wish we could afford. At the end of the day, what matters in creating motivation and earning people's commitment is whether or not they know that you genuinely give them recognition and support, invest in them, care about them as people, and treat them with dignity and respect.

Some leaders, and even some companies, have tried to become more efficient at tapping into this source of motivation by legislating and systematizing their intrinsic rewards. They develop schedules for leadership team members to go out and pat people on the back, or they recognize the employee of the month, which in turn causes everyone else to feel less than special. Suffice it to say that the moment you systematize recognition, it begins to take on the same characteristics of extrinsic rewards, and over time it only serves the purpose of dissatisfying people when they don't receive it.

The Bottom Line:

As leaders, we often have a subconscious or covert entitlement mentality. We believe that people in our organizations owe us their full commitment, when in fact, the truth is that all people owe us is their compliance; if we want their commitment, we must earn it. This realization causes us to stop blaming people for not being fully engaged, and instead look for and discover ways that we can create an environment in which people freely offer their commitment to go beyond the call of duty.

Reflection Questions:

1. Do you find yourself complaining about people not being motivated and committed?

2. Do you know what your team members are motivated by individually?

3. Are you intentional about utilizing intrinsic rewards, such as informal recognition, to demonstrate your genuine appreciation for your employees?

Recommended Follow-up Action:

1. Declare yourself "The One" who is personally responsible for creating an environment in which everyone offers up their commitment.

2. Make it your business to learn what is important to your team members.

3. Be intentional about committing personalized, unpredictable, and authentic acts of recognition and caring toward your team members.

4. Encourage your team members to do the same with everyone else by actively role-modeling what you expect of them.

5. When administering pay increases and other forms of extrinsic rewards, place much of your effort and emphasis on the delivery and the message behind the tangible reward. Remember that it is not what you give them, but what they make it mean and how it makes them feel that matters most.

LESSON 14

What Conversation are You Avoiding?

"Our work, our relationships, and our lives succeed or fail one conversation at a time." - Susan Scott

This is one of my favorite questions to ask in coaching conversations, because I know that 99% of the time the conversation we are avoiding holds the key to freedom and to the achievement of major breakthroughs in our relationships, both professional and personal.

We have all figured out that we can't fight every battle in our lives. Sometimes you just have to grin and bear it. Sometimes it is best to just accept that things are the way they are and move on. It is true that accepting our circumstances often empowers us to channel our energy toward causes that really matter to us; the trouble is that we often fool ourselves, and try to fool others, into thinking that we have truly accepted an unfavorable situation, when in fact we haven't. We also, at times, talk ourselves out of dealing with a situation that needs our attention and try to convince ourselves that it would be useless to try to be complete with it. This causes us to carry the burden of dysfunctional relationships and act like it is not a problem.

Just like trying to move a rock in our shoe to just the right place as we are running, we try to avoid the issue that we know we must deal with by going around it. We convince ourselves that it is not a big deal and we justify this because we have plenty of experience with continuing to succeed and achieve in spite of the dysfunctional relationships in our lives. Unfortunately, just like the rock comes back with a vengeance and pokes us in the ball of our foot, so do the issues we try to avoid.

I do believe you need to pick your battles and recognize that there is a time and place for just letting things go, even if they haven't quite worked out to your satisfaction. But, many of us allow a wedge to be driven between ourselves and our colleagues, our spouses, our parents, or our friends, that sabotages our relationships. Worse yet, the burden of sticking our heads in the sand and pretending the problem is not there often weighs us down and significantly diminishes our quality of life beyond those specific relationships.

Some of the greatest breakthroughs I have witnessed in the lives of people have happened as a direct result of them having had the conversation they had been avoiding. I have seen people who have been through years of therapy simply pick up the phone and call their estranged parent, spouse, or friend, and suddenly feel the kind of liberation they hadn't experienced in years. If you have ever experienced this in the least bit, you know what I am talking about.

The most popular initial response I get to the question regarding the specific conversation someone is avoiding is complete denial. Next come the excuses that usually have to do with not having time or having too much to do to deal with the issue at the moment. This, of course, is hardly ever the real reason because we all know that if something is important to us, we will find the time to do it. If you don't get your paycheck or don't get your invoice paid by a client when you are supposed to, you will find time to make a few calls, but if you don't want to deal with the issue you will find an excuse. What often causes our hesitation to get in action and resolve the issue is that we are unsure of how it will turn out. We imagine the worst outcome and conclude that not taking action is the best route. These imaginary outcomes, however, are often not natural consequences of the actions we know we should take.

I usually don't interact with the reasons a client states for not being in action. Rather than trying to convince them that they do have time if they really want to, or using other arguments to prove that their reason is merely an excuse, I urge them to be unreasonable. Being unreasonable means to act even though you have a reason not to. Whether the reason is legitimate or not doesn't matter. What matters is to get in action in the face of that real or imaginary reason not to.

Having said that, there is one argument that I have heard that seems to stop many people from taking the plunge, and that is that they don't trust themselves to deliver the message in a way that produces a positive outcome. They see themselves confronting the other person, imagine the possible reaction, and figure it is not even worth it to try. In that vein, I'd like to suggest a much more effective and empowering approach to resolving conflict that involves five simple steps.

Of course, the most important ingredient in making this work is a genuine desire to resolve the conflict and achieve a win-win solution. Without that, there is no technique that will achieve sustainable results. In fact, if your motives are not genuine, the fancier your technique, the more you will be perceived as trying to manipulate the other person. Assuming that you do have a genuine desire to resolve the conflict, I'd like you to consider that the conversation should follow the steps I have outlined below:

1. Acknowledge your inauthenticities and take responsibility. A good place to start is to admit that you have had a concern for quite some time, but you have avoided having the conversation you are about to have. Acknowledge that you have used a variety of excuses to avoid the conversation and make a commitment to be forthright in the future.

2. State the issue briefly and ask for the other person's perspective. Then, genuinely listen and look for understanding of their point of view. Save your responses and suggestions for later. If the other person tries to draw you into a debate, only answer the questions you are asked, and do not elaborate on your position and why you feel that way. Instead, get back to asking them questions and allowing them to explain their position.

3. Identify and point out what you both agree on. If the other person brings up areas of disagreement, go back to step 2 and seek to understand.

4. Once you have understood their position and established the areas of agreement, bring up the key topics that you disagree about and begin to work toward a common position. Go for "win-win," or agree to disagree without holding a grudge. At any point, if the other person gets emotional or you sense they feel they are not being heard, go back to step 2.

5. End the conversation with either a commitment from you and the other person, or an agreement to get back together to discuss further.

This approach is much more effective than what normally happens, for a number of reasons:

- There is nothing more disarming than someone that you consider to be a rival or opponent coming to you in a totally non-threatening way.

- Drama loves company. When someone is looking to pick a fight and get into an argument, if the same is not reciprocated, the drama eventually dies down and creates space for rational conversation.

- Creating a base of understanding and finding common ground always makes for a sound foundation to build on.

- As you go through this process, you can separate the agreements and disagreements that may not have been obvious before. You also tend to pick the top issues that you disagree about to discuss, rather than every little thing that may or may not be important in the grand scheme of things.

- People often stay stuck on repeating their point of view and refuse to look for common ground because they don't feel understood. By listening and acknowledging, you not only reduce the intensity of the emotion involved in the discussion, but you also liberate the person to get beyond what they have been hung up on by affirming to them that their point of view has been understood.

- Importantly, this conversation lays the ground work for future conversations going a lot better. The person is less likely to hesitate as much to discuss their disagreements with you in the future, and who knows, they might pick up a tip or two from you on how to handle conflict in the process.

Like any other method, the magic is not in the steps that are listed here, rather it is in your attitude, demeanor, and who you show up as in the other person's world. The few guidelines that are important in effectively adopting this style of conflict management are as follows:

- Stop making the other person wrong and take full responsibility for how the conversation will turn out. Don't give yourself license to blame them if it doesn't go well.

- Pick a time and place that is conducive to having a productive conversation.

- Use your own language and speak from the heart.

- Remain genuinely committed to coming to a common agreement.

- Don't make the other person's reaction mean anything about you. Focus on the topic. If you catch yourself being defensive, be intentional about not acting on your emotions.

The Bottom Line:

Most of the conversations we have during the course of conducting business are focused on solving problems, addressing issues, and getting things done. A small percentage of our conversations have to do with how effective we are at doing all of those things. Working on the system often takes the backseat to working in the system, primarily because for one reason or another, we avoid the conversations that we know we need to have. Knowing why this is and how we can remedy it will have a profound impact on our effectiveness.

Reflection Questions:

1. What conversation(s) are you avoiding?

2. What has kept you from taking the steps to have that conversation?

3. Which parts of your answers to question #2 are natural consequences which will happen for sure, and which ones are your assumptions?

4. What is in it for you, the other person, or the organization or your community if you have the conversation and it goes well?

 Recommended Follow-up Action:

1. Pick one conversation that you have been avoiding and make it happen in the next 24 hours.

2. In your everyday routine, when you suspect that there is disagreement in a conversation, rather than allowing it to fester and parting ways without resolving the issue, use the approach described in this section to find common ground and identify areas of disagreement, and work to resolve them immediately before they become a big issue.

3. Solicit the help of a coach or an accountability partner who is willing to be honest with you to answer the questions listed above objectively, and chart a path forward.

4. As you take action, enjoy your newfound liberation!

The Power of Paradox

"You are doomed to make choices. This is life's greatest paradox."
- Wayne Dyer

I find paradoxes fascinating. I have found that when and if I am able to embrace two seemingly opposite ideas simultaneously, to hold on to one without letting go of the other, I get exposed to a world of possibility that I didn't know existed.

Take some of the concepts I have already talked about in this book, like Servant Leadership, for example. There are plenty of people out there who have never thought about leadership and servanthood going together. They may subscribe to the idea that you can be one or the other, but not both. What about keeping the passion and ditching the drama when it seems that the source of both is that we care deeply about something? How about "I am 'The One' and it's not about me?" That one is definitely a paradox to the naked eye.

If I am "The One," then it had better be about me, and if it is not about me, then how can I be "The One?" There are plenty of so-called leaders who could easily subscribe to only one of the two concepts here. We all know plenty of those who think of themselves as "The One" and expect everyone else to get that, hence making it all about them. They are the ones who will tell you that if they want your opinion, they'll give it to you. It is their way, or the highway. Their motto is, "I am 'The One' and it is all about me and you'd better get that, or else!" Then there are others who get that it is not about them, but they also don't take on the responsibility of being "The One." They are subject to their environment, and although they may be humble and willing to be servants, they do not show up as leaders.

The truth is that none of the approaches described above can be effective for servant leaders because if it is all about you, you can't be a good servant, and if you are not "The One," you can't lead others. Keep in mind, I am not referring to styles here. I have seen servant leaders who are outspoken, and I have seen ones who are fairly low-key, depending on their temperament and tendency to be an introvert or an extrovert. Servant Leadership is expressed in a variety of styles. What I am talking about here is the ability to embrace both sides of a paradox, no matter how it is expressed.

By now, you have probably figured out that I am a big fan of metaphors. When it comes to paradoxes, I think of a jar of oil and vinegar. There is a plane that separates the two liquids. If you imagine yourself being a tiny molecule in that jar, if you are positioned just exactly on that plane where you are touched on one side by oil and the other by vinegar, then you get the benefit of the paradox. If you are slightly off, you are immersed in one or the other. I am sure I have lost the chemists among us who are thinking of what kind of molecule they would have to be to actually float on that plane and so on. Suffice it to say, chemistry was not my strongest subject in school so let's move on.

In reality, I believe most of us will have our moments when we lean more toward one concept than the other in any given paradox, but what is important is whether or not our behavior demonstrates, over time, that we subscribe to both ideas. I also believe that when we are intentional about fully embracing seemingly opposite schools of thought, after a while it becomes second nature. It becomes abundantly clear, for instance, that leadership and servanthood are inseparable, and although certain circumstances may call for more of one or the other, the spirit in which each is expressed is not one of duality, but unity.

Consider these other paradoxes and what they might make available to you if you could fully embrace them:

- 100% contentment with *what is,* and 100% tenacity to create *what can be.*

- 100% commitment to winning, and zero attachment to the scoreboard.

- 100% honesty in expressing disagreement with an idea, and not making the other person wrong for subscribing to the idea.

- Learning from the past, leaving the baggage in the past and being present.

- Planning for the future, and not worrying about it and being present.

- Having a high sense of urgency, and remaining calm the whole time.

- Being liberated to be oneself, and having the discipline to conform to the established standards of the organization.

- Hating the sin, and loving the sinner (no matter how you define sin according to your belief system).

- Being completely confident in your ideas and beliefs, and remaining open to new ideas and opportunities for improvement.

- Taking full responsibility for everything, and not blaming yourself for how things turn out.

As you look at the list, some of these may make more sense than others. There may be some that may not even seem like paradoxes to you because you have had some practice embracing them for some time. Yet, there may be others that either represent a contradiction or may even seem impossibly strange and unclear to you. This is where your opportunity lies.

I realized a few years ago that I was living an "either/or" life, and as I looked at various aspects of my life, I found plenty of evidence that I had made choices based on assumptions that were simply not true. Assumptions like, "I can either excel at work or be a good father," or, "I can either be respectful or truthful," or, "I can either empathize with a person I am coaching or tell them what they need to hear." I can go on and on, and I am certain that I have several more of these assumptions still running in my life. But, I am glad to say that when I discovered that some of these were just stories I had made up about myself and my life, I was able to let go and take on a "have your cake and eat it too" approach. I have experienced profound joy and freedom as a result of the paradoxes I have been able to embrace.

The Bottom Line:

We often live "either/or" lives and miss the opportunity to embrace two seemingly opposite ideas, and consequently seize the opportunity to be intentional about having the best of both worlds.

Discovering the power of paradoxes creates a powerful incentive for exploring the possibilities that we thought impossible in the past.

 Reflection Questions:

1. Do you have an "either/or" mentality?

2. Are there any of the paradoxes on the list that seem unclear or strange to you?

3. Have you ever come to a realization that two seemingly opposite or competing ideas could coexist?

4. Could you benefit from embracing any of the paradoxes that are listed?

5. If there are any aspects of leadership that you are struggling with, can you think of an underlying dualistic or "either/or" assumption that is holding you back?

 Recommended Follow-up Action:

1. Consider the concepts listed in this section and look into your personal and professional life to see where your bias toward one side of the paradox or the other shows up. Consider how it is working for you.

2. Discuss any paradoxes that you are unclear about with someone else. Begin exploring what they might mean and how they might apply to you.

3. Identify one area in which you have an "either/or" mentality and begin to practice embracing the idea of an "and" mentality instead.

4. Declare your intentions to embrace a certain paradox with others around you, and ask for their feedback and support in doing so.

Pay the Parking Fee

"Every new beginning comes from some other beginning's end."
- Seneca

I grew up in a middle class family, so I don't have too many memories of having to go without the basic necessities. Sure, there was an occasional disappointment that my brothers or I couldn't have a certain toy or something, but nothing major. When I moved to the US at age 16, my parents were initially able to continue to support me financially, but after a while, due to my own desire to be self-sufficient and difficulties back in my home country of Iran, I began to work for minimum wage or below minimum wage plus tips. As I worked as a dishwasher, busboy, and then a waiter for years to support myself, I basically had no safety net and I had to watch my money very carefully. My wife and I lived within modest means and had three jobs between the two of us as I went to school.

We have come a long way since then and have been abundantly blessed. We can afford many things that we couldn't even dream of back then. But, a few years ago, I had an experience that opened my eyes to how I was still holding on to some of the old paradigms and behaviors that were no longer serving me well.

I was moonlighting as a professional facilitator at the time and had been hired to conduct a one-and-a-half day team-building session for a private equity firm in Atlanta. The session was scheduled for 9am and I was supposed to meet with the meeting sponsor at 8:30am. I pulled up to the building where we were going to have the session at about 8:15am and noticed that the only parking option available was the basement of the 15-story building. I pulled into the parking garage only to find out that there would be a $15 parking fee, which I didn't want to pay.

After a few seconds of quick thinking, I remembered that there were some outdoor parking lots a few blocks down from the building and decided I would take my chances with those since I still had ten minutes or so left. I drove out of the garage and went looking for cheaper parking and I felt very smart when I saw the sign that advertised a $5 parking fee for the whole day.

I have to admit that the parking lot was a bit farther away than I had thought, and the worse news was that it had started drizzling! I parked the car, grabbed my briefcase, and started heading for the building a few blocks down. The light drizzle turned to rain and my strides grew longer and faster. Time was running short. I did make it to the office right at 8:30am, but I was drenched and out of breath and had to think fast about what I was going to say when they asked me why I didn't just park in the basement parking garage.

Fortunately, the meeting sponsor was a very nice man and he and I had a great conversation; I was able to quickly gain my composure, and we had a very successful session. On the way home that evening, it all of a sudden hit me that I was still acting like I did when I was working for minimum wage, even though they were paying me thousands of dollars for a one-and-a-half day engagement. I had more money but had kept the same mentality.

I got clear on that day that the level of frugality that helped me survive in my younger days was no longer necessary or serving a purpose in my life. In fact, it was keeping me in bondage and would potentially sabotage my ability to excel further if I did not let it go. I had not even given it a second thought that I could now afford to pay $15 for parking, and that I needed to let go of that minor issue and all the hassle that came with it. It was like someone poured a bucket of ice water on my head. I realized on that day that some of the beliefs, limiting thoughts, and assumptions I was dragging with me into my future no longer fit. It was like I was going to a formal ball in a tuxedo, but still wearing my old sneakers.

Since that day, I have found myself questioning and examining what I hold to be true, and I have discovered many other opportunities to let go and set myself free from a way of thinking and being that may have served a purpose at one point, but does not any longer.

The Bottom Line:

Holding on to paradigms and habits that were created at some point in our lives and dragging them with us has a pervasive impact on whether we are able to fully embrace the potential of our new circumstances and capabilities. Being intentional about discovering the hidden ways in which we sabotage ourselves empowers us to expose and eliminate these invisible culprits.

 ## Reflection Questions:

1. Are there habits that you developed earlier in your career or life that you are holding on to, even though they no longer serve a purpose?

2. Have the people around you, especially those close to you, been trying to tell you that you need to let go of some of your old paradigms?

3. Are you open to examining your beliefs and habits with a fresh set of eyes, and are you willing to make adjustments?

 Recommended Follow-up Action:

1. Ask someone close to you for honest feedback to gain insight on the questions posed above.

2. Begin to examine areas of your life where you experience stress or deliver sub-optimum results, and look for habits or beliefs that you could change.

If You Can't Run, Walk

"The secret to getting ahead is getting started."
- Mark Twain

If you've read Lesson 3, *Transformative Realizations Have an Expiration Date*, you'll remember me telling you about my experience of trying to become a runner by reading a book. When it finally sank in that I had to actually get out and run, I began my training with the intention to run 5 kilometers without stopping. I didn't care how long it took, I just wanted to be able to do it, because even that accomplishment represented a huge victory over the past for me.

On most days, my wife and I would go out for a walk/jog either in the morning before I went off to work, or in the evening after I got back from work. For about two weeks, I followed my plan and was out there walking/jogging three to four times a week. Then, for the next few weeks I did nothing and had tons of excuses for not being in action. Then, I got back in the saddle again and went out walking/jogging with my wife.

On one particular occasion, I was jogging up a hill with my wife by my side. I noticed that she was keeping up with me and she was walking! That is when that little voice in the back of my mind went on a rampage. I was thinking that the only reason I was calling what I was doing "jogging" was so that I could say I was following my plan. I thought, "I should be better at jogging by this point." I started blaming myself for making excuses for a few weeks, and I almost stopped jogging.

Then it dawned on me that all those thoughts were exactly the reason I had never been able to run in my entire life. I'd get out there and feel like I ought to be able to run like a pro in a few days, and when it didn't happen and when I came up on a hill, I'd be disappointed and quit. On this particular day, I didn't do that. I just kept jogging at the speed that I could. I realized that under the circumstances, that was all I could do and if I did

> *"Get out of your head and remain in action no matter how fast or slow you can move."*

that long enough, I'd eventually have more strength and endurance to do better.

In aerobic exercise, it is healthy to achieve and maintain a heart rate that is in the training zone. Anything less than that and you are not building stamina, and more than that, you may be risking a heart attack. Now, depending on your physical condition, one person might need to run a lot faster than someone else to achieve the same level of training, but again the key is to do what you can to push yourself to that next level. When it comes to conquering any kind of challenge in life, what is most important is not necessarily how fast you are going but whether you stay in action or not, and whether you are pushing against the boundaries of your comfort zone.

Disempowering thoughts are bound to show up, and your tendency will be to want to quit, but the best thing to do is get out of your head and remain in action no matter how fast or slow you can move. Otherwise, your old habits will kick in and rob you of your opportunity to stretch yourself to the next level of effectiveness.

The key to achieving success is not the absence of negative thoughts, but the ability to stay in action in the face of those thoughts. In other words, there is nothing wrong with being discouraged sometimes and thinking about quitting. We all do it and it is very natural. It is what you *do* when those thoughts show up that makes the difference. If you are not in action, all there is to do is to get in action. If the circumstances don't allow you to go as fast or make as much progress as you imagined, then go as fast as you can under the circumstances, rather than making yourself or other people wrong and just stopping.

I recognize that this is much easier said than done, but just like any worthy endeavor, you must begin by pondering the idea and then, if it makes sense to you, make a decision to apply it in an area of your life and keep practicing. In some cases, you may choose to no longer pursue a certain goal. In that case, choose that option freely, accept responsibility, and take what you get in terms of consequences.

If you choose to move forward, recognize that you will fall off the wagon, but it is usually not getting off track that does the damage, rather it is staying there and not making the effort to get back on track. When you are on a diet and you make a mistake and take

> *"The key to achieving success is not the absence of negative thoughts, but the ability to stay in action in the face of those thoughts."*

a bite of a brownie, it is not that bite that does the damage, it is the next six brownies after that. You take a bite and figure nobody is going to eat the rest of that one anyway, so you finish the whole thing, and then you figure since you fell of the wagon, you are just not made for this kind of thing, and you go ahead and have a few more. It is great to hold yourself to high standards, but when you fall short, your high standards should cause you to not use your setbacks as an excuse to give up, no matter how much damage has been done already.

Often, we get in action and expect certain results to be produced as a consequence of our action, and when the results fall short of our expectations, we give up. Again, it is great to have a stretching vision of what is possible and what we want to accomplish, but those expectations cannot be used as an excuse for us to not be in action. If you start going to the gym and begin eating right, and you have a certain target for how much weight you want to lose or how much muscle mass you want to gain, and you fall short of the progress you thought you should be making along the way, it doesn't mean that working out and eating right are the wrong things to do. The key is to be committed to achieving the goal, but not attached to it.

Commitment drives you to do the best you can, but attachment causes you to take your eye off the ball and be worried about the scoreboard when you ought to have all of your focus on winning the game. True commitment to winning compels you to play your heart out, no matter what the score is, and if you do that you increase your chances of being rewarded with a favorable score. Sure, it makes sense to keep an eye on the results, make course corrections as appropriate, and set strategies that will help you win, but that's different than letting your results-to-date diminish your best effort in the present.

The Bottom Line:

We often don't get in action because we are waiting for the perfect start, and at times we stop because we are not making the kind of progress we think we should be making. The key to progress is starting exactly where you are and staying in action, no matter how fast or slow you can go.

 ## Reflection Questions:

1. Are there areas of your career or life where you have given up on taking any action simply because you don't see yourself taking action significant enough to make a difference?

2. Are there plans you have put on the back burner because you are not sure if you are going to be great at executing them?

3. Are you holding off on starting something because you are waiting for that perfect start?

4. Have you allowed your disappointment in your results, in any area, to cause you to not do what you know in your heart you ought to be doing?

 ## Recommended Follow-up Action:

1. Write down the answers to the above questions and identify 1 to 2 actions that you know you should be taking to achieve the goals you have set for yourself.

2. Make a commitment that you will get in action and stay in action whether you see any results or not.

3. Identify the specific action you will take and the date by which it will be completed.

4. Declare your intentions to someone who will hold you accountable to doing what you said you would do and help you celebrate when you accomplish your goal.

What Lens are You Looking Through?

"If your actions inspire others to dream more, learn more, do more and become more, you are a leader." - John Quincy Adams

When I came to the US I had a very limited English vocabulary and no clue what to expect. I came over on my own and knew no one. By the grace of God, I made it through a series of trials and tribulations, and was able to get a decent education and enjoy a successful career. I was also fortunate enough to marry a virtuous woman and have two wonderful children. Against the odds, I have had the good fortune of having lived in and travelled to many exotic places around the world, and have had experiences that I could never have dreamt of when I was growing up.

Sometimes, during certain moments of success or fulfillment in my life, I look back and I cannot believe just how far I have come. I wonder how that 16-year old kid managed to be so blessed in so many ways. I also recognize that while I had no clue where I would be at this point in my life when I started my journey, the vision of where I am today was formed along the way as I took baby steps toward my future. I know that my life could have turned out completely different and that who I am, what I do, and what I have today is not just a product of random events in my life, but is heavily influenced by what I considered to be possible at some point.

A few years ago, my wife, kids, and I were on vacation at the beach. We were sitting by the water and enjoying the perfect weather. We started talking about just how blessed we had been in our lives and just how grateful we were for all the opportunities that had come our way. We started envisioning the future, and sharing with each other what we would like to have, be, or do in the years to come. We are big believers in vision boards and the power of seeing ourselves in the future that we would like to experience one day, so we started talking specifically about what we wanted to accomplish.

As we were talking, I noticed a yacht on the water nearby and all of a sudden it hit me. My image of the kind of people who were on that yacht was so different than the image I had of myself. They were rich people and I could not see myself ever being that rich. Not that I am a yacht enthusiast or anything, but it occurred to me that the reason I did not own a yacht like that was because I didn't see myself ever being able to afford something like that.

I have coached people hundreds of times on this concept, but it had never occurred to me at the level that it did on that day, how the limitations I had placed on myself were holding me back from achieving even more than I had in my life. The yacht on the water that day made the picture crystal clear to me. The lens through which I was looking at the world made some things in the distance appear focused, bright and within reach, and others fuzzy and unattainable. Everything I had accomplished up to that point had, at some time, appeared to be achievable, and everything else, like the idea of owning a yacht, had not.

The pervasive effect of what we consider to be possible or not is such that it completely dominates our perception of the world around us. When we write something off and don't consider it probable or even possible, we deny ourselves access to the information and resources that are pertinent to achieving that possibility. We also begin to look at how things are only through the lens of what's probable, and we accept the conditions of certain aspects of our lives as unchangeable. After a while, we get so used to the status quo that we don't even notice that it could be better. In fact, once we determine just how much success we want or deserve, we begin to operate according to that setting, and as long as we have not achieved it, we do all that we can to make it happen. But, as soon as we surpass it or it looks like we are about to, we begin to covertly sabotage ourselves so that we won't go beyond it.

When I was a plant manager, I would often walk around the production floor striking up conversations with machine operators about their image of what was possible. At one time, we desperately needed to elevate our standards on so many fronts and I was using every opportunity to shift people's mindset about how much better we could be. One of the problems I often encountered was that people would leave their tools and other items on top of the machine guards rather than putting them in their place. This was against our standards as it increased the risk of something falling into the product, but since they had done it for years, it seemed normal. This problem would show up on daily and monthly audits, get corrected, and then it would creep back up again.

It was clear that people on the floor were not bought in to the value of doing anything different and all the reasoning in the world about the potential negative impacts of this behavior would not have changed their minds. I am happy to report that we did end up completely transforming our attitude and behavior in this area to the point where visitors would consistently praise us as one of the cleanest and most orderly facilities they had seen. What it took was not the constant badgering of people about the standard, but the shifting of their own internal standard and the lens through which they were looking at the situation.

This was accomplished through many discussions and conversations. One that I still remember to this day and I have reapplied in many cases went like this: I walked up to one of the guys that was running a wrapper on the floor and, as usual, he had a bunch of tools and supplies on his machine. Rather than confronting the issue head-on and getting into the normal conversations that had produced no permanent results, I decided to take a different approach.

We had set a goal to be "The Showcase of Excellence" and I had been going around sharing my positive predictions about our future with as many people as I could. I would tell them that we would be featured in the Atlanta Journal Constitution, which is the main newspaper in Atlanta, and things like that—which, by the way, eventually happened. At that stage, not too many people believed that it would actually happen, but the idea that it might be possible for us to deliver some extraordinary results was beginning to take hold.

In any case, on this particular day, I said to the wrapper operator, "Can you imagine that a year from now, we are going to be invited to a banquet hosted by the mayor of Atlanta to honor us as the best manufacturing facility in the city?" He smiled as if to humor me and go along with the idea. I asked, "What if they asked us to nominate one person to receive the award from the mayor and I were to nominate you? Imagine yourself on that stage receiving an award on our behalf, while your family and friends are cheering you on in the audience." By this time, the imagery was actually beginning to take shape; I could tell that he was seeing it in his mind's eye. Then I said, "Now, imagine that they asked us to bring one picture that they would project on the screen in the background to show just how high our standards are while you receive that award." Before he could figure out where I was going with that, I hit him with the question that permanently shifted his thinking to a higher level in an instant. You probably guessed it. The question was, "Would you want to put a picture of this wrapper up on that screen to represent our standards of excellence?"

Of course, we were having fun with this conversation and it wasn't all that serious, but I can tell you that it made a huge difference in the way he looked at his work area from that point forward. For a moment, it seemed as if he was seeing the mess for the first time and indeed he was, because he was

"You cannot see what's possible looking through the lens of what is okay."

now looking at his machine through a completely different lens, the lens of excellence. He was finally seeing the gap between reality and what was possible. He was bought in and the problem was solved.

Naturally, there were many other people in different parts of the plant who had to get this, but the movement had to start with me having similar conversations with as many people as I could. I very quickly saw that once I started looking at things through the lens of excellence and I stopped tolerating them as "good enough," others got on board and they became advocates for the same cause. I have countless examples of permanent shifts like this that happened, which culminated in us dramatically improving our results and morale in that plant.

Since then, I have used this approach to effectively help people see that the lens they are looking through is causing them to perpetuate mediocrity. They can't see *what's possible* looking through the lens of *what is okay*. They promote what they permit and perpetuate mediocrity without realizing that they hold the key to transformation.

The Bottom Line:

The standards you set for yourself and your organization create the context for how the current state occurs to people. Painting a clear picture of what's possible and having everyone embrace it as their own vision compels them to get in action toward creating the desired future. A stretching vision is energizing. It not only reveals the gaps and discrepancies in a different light, it also provides a worthwhile reason to persevere.

Reflection Questions:

1. Are there areas of your life, personally or professionally, in which you have been stagnant for a while?

2. If you were not limited by the external barriers or your internal limitations, what future would you want to create?

3. What is the reason you have not created that future? What limiting thoughts or perceived barriers are holding you back?

4. Are you deliberate about regularly challenging your assumptions about yourself and your capabilities?

5. When was the last time you consciously examined and expanded your vision of what is possible?

6. Are you intentional about causing your team members to get excited about a future that inspires them?

Recommended Follow-up Action:

1. Make a list of the things you would like to do or have in your life.

2. Pick one item and record your thoughts on that subject. This is best accomplished by writing down or typing, non-stop, all the random thoughts that are floating around in your head. At this point, don't worry about organizing your thoughts. Just write them down.

3. Go through your notes and underline the key themes in your assumptions about the situation or yourself.

4. Ask yourself if those assumptions are true, or if they are things that you made up about yourself at some point.

5. Identify a few assumptions that you are willing to challenge and write down the new paradigm you are going to take on.

6. Identify actions you plan to take based on your new paradigm, and commit to getting them completed by a certain date.

7. Get in action!

8. Repeat this exercise regularly with other items on your list.

Respect Doesn't Cost a Thing

"I speak to everyone in the same way, whether he is the garbage man or the president of the university." - Albert Einstein

I spend a great deal of my time on the road, and I am on two to four flights almost every week. Normally, I fly coach but sometimes, due to my frequent flyer status or simply because very few people in their right mind book tickets to fly at some of the odd times when I travel, I have the good fortune of being upgraded to first class. That represents a real treat when you are generally squished into a smaller seat, trying to make sure that your knees don't bump the seat in front of you too many times. So, when I do get upgraded, I am very happy to have the experience of priority boarding, wider seats, better snacks, and free drinks if I choose to partake.

All of these perks are nice, but that is not all you get in first class. Generally, you also get a more experienced flight attendant who has done their time in coach and seems to be just as happy as you are not to be back there. You get more polite greetings and the kind of chit-chat that is intended to communicate that they are happy you are there. And, if you happen to be struggling with putting your luggage up in the overhead compartment, someone will help you or they might even take it and put it in the closet up front. All in all, most of the time, you get the kind of customer service that is far superior to what you get in coach. Out of embarrassment, I tend to avoid eye contact with the "poor souls" passing by to take their place in coach where, most of the time, none of the good stuff I mentioned happens.

To be clear, this is not an indictment against the hard working and courteous flight attendants out there who are doing what they can to perform their duties. I have come across numerous flight attendants in coach who have gone above and beyond the call of duty to make the passengers feel welcome and comfortable. So, exceptions to what I have described do exist, but I am talking about my experience in general.

I am also not suggesting that things ought to be equal in those two classes of travel. If I have paid two to three times as much for a plane ticket, I ought to get better food and amenities. That makes perfect sense and is good business. The issue is that some of the stuff available in first class doesn't cost anything and could easily be extended to the people in coach. An intentional smile, eye contact, and special greeting are not commodities that should be reserved for those who have paid more for their seat. Extending a certain level of respect for someone who cannot fit their carry-on in the overhead compartment ought to be a basic courtesy extended to all passengers. I understand that it is harder to chit-chat with 100 people if you are serving the coach cabin than it is if you are serving 12 people up front, but even if you have time to talk to five people, how you treat them speaks volumes to everyone else around.

The question comes down to what we consider to be common courtesy and respect that must be extended to all and what treatment we consider to be a privilege for the few. Unfortunately, many of us have, consciously or unconsciously, established conditions for how we treat different types of people.

These conditions may be based on someone's position in the organization, their wealth, education, and many other factors. The problem this causes in organizations is that it divides us into "us and them" and, "haves and have nots."

Again, to be clear, I am not advocating that every person in the organization have the same perks and benefits that the CEO has. In fact, in my experience, people are quite willing to accept the differences that are justified. If and when you hear complaints about those things not being fair, it is only because leaders have driven a wedge between themselves and the organization. When people do not trust and respect the competence or character of their leaders, they tend to lash out at them whichever way they can. Otherwise, most people are reasonable in understanding that the company must provide certain levels of compensation to senior leaders in order to attract and retain the right caliber of leadership.

It is when we go too far and start withholding the basic human courtesies that true dissatisfaction and resentment begin to emerge. It is when we have things like assigned parking spots and exclusive lunch rooms that people begin to believe that their leaders think they are better than them. The signs of this kind of double standard are everywhere around us if we care enough to look for them.

If we take the time to inquire about these subtle or sometimes overt forms of institutional and legalistic discrimination, and put ourselves in other people's shoes, it is easy to see how we would feel on the other side. I have found that identifying and addressing visible signs of inequality goes a long way in demonstrating a leader's true commitment to the organization; even the smallest effort, if genuine, will cause people to go beyond mere compliance and offer their true commitment.

One of the visible signs of this practice in many organizations is the removal of time clocks, demonstrating trust that the hourly employees will document their time accurately, just like we expect the salaried employees to communicate if they are not going to be at work. Over the years, I have heard many arguments against this approach such as, "We are legally bound to have documentation of people being at work," or, "Hourly people get paid by the hour, so we need to know how many hours they worked, whereas the salaried people get paid for delivering results." I have personally been able to prove all these arguments to be null and void, and just excuses to maintain the status quo primarily because leaders don't see the value of the de-stigmatization it brings versus the risk that someone may cheat the system. There are plenty of organizations that have figured out a way to do it without violating any laws and it has paid significant dividends.

Another common practice I have seen at manufacturing facilities is to have separate entrances for employees. There is a nice and clean one for the higher-ups, and a dark and dingy one for the "workers." Again, there may be certain situations when some of these distinctions are necessary or even required, but in most cases they are purely driven by management's desire to preserve some level of exclusivity, to the ultimate detriment of the morale of the organization.

I remember a story that was repeatedly told at a facility I worked at a few years back that illustrates this type of discrimination to the extreme. It was about an incident that had happened many years earlier, but the impact was so profound that it had been etched in people's collective memory. According to several people who told me the same story, the company was having a Christmas lunch at the workplace and the temporary employees had not been invited. Apparently, one temporary employee showed up because he did not realize he wasn't supposed to be there. The temp went through the line and fixed himself a plate and just as he was getting ready to sit down to eat his lunch, the manager approached him. He took his plate, threw it in the trash in front of everyone, and admonished the guy for crashing the party, and basically kicked him out of the lunch room. The manager's justification for his behavior was that the company didn't want to take a chance on being sued for co-employment. In case you are not familiar with this term, simply put, co-employment laws protect people from working side-by-side with others and getting paid significantly less. Therefore, companies have a *de facto* practice of distinguishing between their regular employees and temporary workforce to avoid being sued.

As it relates to this particular story, I am 100% sure that the manager's behavior did far more damage than would have been done had he allowed the situation to play out. First of all, the possibility of a temporary employee eating a Christmas lunch and then using that as grounds to sue the employer for co-employment are infinitesimally small. Secondly, even if the temp had been required to eat his lunch elsewhere, the situation could have been handled with much more tact and courtesy and without public embarrassment for the employee; I am certain that the manager would not have treated his boss that way if the boss had deviated from a standard. The humiliation he caused the temp indeed cost him his credibility within the organization, and caused more damage over the years than allowing the temp to eat his lunch ever would have.

Transformative Leaders who are committed to bringing out the best in people get everyone involved in delivering extraordinary results. They look for, and find, ways to eliminate the differences in how people are treated such that everyone feels validated and valued for what they bring, and they are motivated to bring their best to the team.

The Bottom Line:

We tend to classify people into categories and treat them according to how we think the people in that category should be treated. This serves us well when it comes to ensuring that legitimate distinctions in responsibility and compensation are made according to capability and contributions. However, when we blur the line between these legitimate considerations and common courtesy and respect, we tend to widen the gap between the "haves" and "have nots," and alienate large numbers of people in the organization.

Reflection Questions:

1. Have you ever felt that you were treated differently based on how *important* someone perceived you to be?

2. What do you think of a person who is super nice and respectful toward their boss, but does not extend the same courtesy toward their subordinates?

3. Do you treat people differently based on their rank and position in the organization or society?

4. How do you think the people in your organization perceive you as it relates to question #3?

5. Do the policies and cultural norms in your organization create distinctions between different classes of people?

Recommended Follow-up Action:

1. Pay attention to how you greet people and notice whether you behave differently toward people based on their position.

2. Ask people for their honest opinion on your behavior and attitude as it relates to point #1, above.

3. Take note of the cultural artifacts and visible signs that exist in your organization that divide people into classes.

4. Identify 1 to 2 visible ways in which you are going to send a strong signal to the organization that you are interested in ensuring that everyone is treated with respect and dignity, no matter what their position is.

LESSON 20

Just Be It!

"I AM, two of the most powerful words; for what you put after them shapes your reality." - Anonymous

Let's face it, this happens to the best of us: We are constantly subject to the vicious cycle of our circumstances determining our attitude, and our attitude influencing our actions in a way that creates more of the circumstances we don't want. Unless you are intentional and committed to resetting your attitude and acting on your commitments as opposed to the emotions associated with the current situation, you will find yourself in a self-fulfilling prophecy of predicting a negative future, acting according to it, and then bringing it about.

Oftentimes we set a goal and give it what we consider to be our best shot with the expectation to see some results, and when the results don't show up, we change the course of our actions and sabotage ourselves. The simplest example of this is something that I have personally experienced. It has to do with physical exercise. On several occasions in my life, I have set goals in this area and started working out, only to be disappointed when a few weeks into it, I couldn't see the results I was expecting to see. I'd let my disappointment get the best of me and reduce the intensity of my effort and the quality of my commitment.

The key to reversing this effect when you notice it is happening, of course, is to continue to behave based on your commitment, not your circumstance. Another way to look at it is to let your attitude be what it would be if you had already achieved what you're after. Can you imagine what that would be like? It would mean that if you were just passed over for the promotion you really wanted, your attitude would be to operate as if you had gotten the promotion anyway.

I know this is much easier said than done, but just hang in there with me for a moment. I think you would agree that if you're committed to getting promoted, it would be better to set yourself up for the next opportunity than to let your disappointment determine your attitude and behavior. You might be thinking, "It is hard to do this," and I won't deny that, but assuming you remain committed to the cause, it can be done. History has shown us numerous examples of how people achieved extraordinary results against all odds. Gandhi's triumph against the British empire, Helen Keller's accomplishments in the face of severe disabilities, and Nelson Mandela's victory in abolishing apartheid and his rise to the presidency of the very country in which he was denied the right to vote, to name a few.

Let's use a scenario where you want to lose a few pounds. Let's say you begin to work out and eat right, and a few weeks later you still don't see any results, or at least not to the extent you expected to see. The question to ask at that point is, if you were fit and thin already, would you want to go back to being out of shape? If you were there already, what would you do or not do to maintain what you had? Would you be willing to continue to eat right? Would you be willing to work out regularly? You would probably be more likely to continue to do those things to maintain what you had if you were there already. Isn't it harder to take a leap of faith and do those things hoping you will get some results someday? Sure it is.

Have you ever found yourself thinking, "Of course, it is easy for Warren Buffett to give away millions of dollars because he is rich!" or, "It is easy for Joe to have a positive attitude because he already got his promotion!?" The trouble is that our default mode thinking leads us to get the cause and effect mixed up. We think somebody is generous with their giving because they are rich. It doesn't occur to us that they may be rich because they have a giving spirit, and that they were probably giving generously even when they didn't have much money.

The point is that it is always easier to see yourself *doing* what rich people do if you could already see yourself *being* as rich as they are. It is easier to *do* what fit people do if you see yourself *being* fit and in shape. If you are being rich, you do rich people stuff and that leads to you being rich. If you see yourself as successful, you behave as successful people do and you attract success in your life. People who are successful often already have an abundance mentality as opposed to a scarcity mentality. They cause others to be successful, rather than being afraid that someone else's success may diminish their own chances.

There is a difference between behaving as if you were already successful, and behaving as if you want to be successful someday. Let me explain. A friend of mine was looking for a plant manager job, which would have been a promotion for him. He called me and asked for coaching as he was not being very successful in his search. The biggest piece of advice I had for him was to walk into the interview *being a plant manager*, not being the operations manager who wanted to be a plant manager! This advice served him well, as he received an offer for a plant manager role shortly after that.

You might be thinking, "How can I act as if I am already there when I don't have the power, authority, or the finances that come with being there?" I am, of course, not suggesting that you go out and write a check for a million dollars when you only have a thousand dollars in your account, or make the decisions that your boss would make, before you get promoted. What you can do, however, is shift your attitude, thoughts, and words, and you'll be amazed at the results you see. You will find that some of your actions and your daily routines will shift in the direction of the kinds of actions and habits that those people who are already there exhibit.

Envision yourself being there now and begin to examine your thoughts, words, actions, and habits through the lens of what the rich or fit or successful version of you would do. This naturally lines you up with that way of being and you will soon have what you want to have. The beauty of this approach is that even if it takes a long time for you to get there, you will be living into the future that you anticipate, and that transforms your experience of your journey in every moment along the way.

The Bottom Line:

We act according to how we relate to ourselves. If we relate to ourselves with limited thinking about what's possible, we act according to it and bring it about. But, if we envision ourselves having already achieved what we are targeting for, we behave according to that and bring about a different outcome.

Reflection Questions:

1. Can you think of a specific situation where you are behaving according to the emotions caused by your circumstances rather than your commitment?

2. What is the source of your emotions? Is it fear of an unfavorable outcome in the future? Is it regret about past events that have led to the current situation?

3. Would you be more effective at *doing* whatever needs to be done to change your circumstances if you were *being* confident and hopeful rather than worried and fearful?

4. Can you imagine everything having turned out the way you wished it would?

5. If that were the case, how would you be feeling? What would you be doing?

 Recommended Follow-up Action:
1. Complete the exercise titled **"Restoring Power"** in the appendix.

FINAL THOUGHTS

Looks like you made it to the end of the book! I hope the way you got here was not by going all the way to the end to get to the summary. You may have read every section, or skipped around and read the topics of immediate interest, but no matter how you got here, I'd like to thank you for your commitment to being, and showing up as the Transformative Leader that you are. I hope that you have picked up a few golden nuggets of wisdom in this book that have been helpful to you already. I also hope that you will revisit this book from time to time as you continue to move forward in your journey, so that other nuggets will be revealed and gleam out from familiar territory as you reread it again and again.

Ideally, the combination of how I have presented the ideas and how you have processed them has resulted in you recognizing that leadership is not nearly as complicated as we make it out to be. In fact, it is fairly simple and it comes down to the following:

1. Your 100% commitment to a cause that inspires you.

2. Your willingness to declare yourself "The One" who is going to make a difference.

3. Your courage to be humble and look inward for what is in the way of progress.

4. Your awareness of the automatic thought patterns and attitudes that are holding you back.

5. Your intentionality to consistently make course corrections in your behavior.

6. Your knowledge of tools and methodologies that increase your effectiveness as a leader.

7. Your ability to use the tools and techniques in a context that fulfills your commitment.

Just because something is simple, however, doesn't mean it's easy. On the contrary, the challenge of taking my leadership effectiveness to the next level has been the most difficult thing I have personally ever taken on. The reason being that the first five factors I listed above don't necessarily happen naturally, and the ways of the world and our own uncontrolled tendencies work against these manifesting in our lives even when we do make the effort to cultivate them. We have been conditioned to be partially committed. We have the tendency to think someone bigger and better than us ought to be "The One." We tend to look "out there" for problems and solutions, rather than within ourselves. Our automatic thoughts and destructive attitudes have been with us for so long that we think they are part of who we are. We make course corrections in our behavior, but after a few tries we begin to make ourselves or other people wrong and give in. Unfortunately, the world we live in and our education system is designed, by default, to perpetuate these tendencies rather than cultivate more productive ones.

That's why developing the mindset and adopting the behaviors of Transformative Leadership feels difficult at first. This is also why most leadership development efforts focus on gaining knowledge and developing the ability to use tools and techniques; these are by far the easiest parts of the process, but simply going after more knowledge and stopping short of taking on the tough stuff doesn't carry the day. What separates Transformative Leaders from the rest is their commitment to practicing and mastering those first five factors.

I sincerely hope that your experience of reading this book and putting the concepts into practice has helped you begin to cultivate all of these characteristics in yourself in a way that matters to you and those who count on you to lead them. If you were able to see something that was hidden from your view and feel inspired, I'd urge you to act on your inspiration. Declare your intentions to others and inspire them to see something for themselves. If you are finding all of this overwhelming, and if you are making yourself wrong for not having seen the light, and if you feel yourself wanting to give up on the idea that these concepts can work for you, then you are at the crossroads where you get to choose the path you are going to take.

If this is you, I'd encourage you to read OPL #17 titled, "If You Can't Run, Walk," and reflect on the next small step you can take in your journey. You don't have to commit to a giant leap and take on all the characteristics and behaviors of Transformative Leaders all at once. Start with one small commitment and declare yourself "The One." Look inward and identify one thing that is sabotaging your progress and be intentional about getting back on track when—not if—you fall off the wagon again. Go at your own pace and get some small victories under your belt and celebrate your wins, rather than focusing on how much further you have to go.

I have provided a tool in the appendix, called the **"Transformation Blueprint"** that is designed to assist you in mapping out the transformation you are committed to causing. I encourage you to complete the exercise as soon as possible. If you are skeptical as to whether it would work for you or not, I have good news for you: Enthusiasm is not a pre-requisite to get started! Just the mere choice to take the path of being in action already separates you from the rest, and that choice alone will begin to put you back in touch with the Transformative Leader that is, and will always be, inside of you.

With that, I wish you the very best as you *boldly declare, courageously pursue, and abundantly achieve the extraordinary!*

APPENDIX

Restoring Power

1. What is not working, or not working as well as you want it to? (Results that are not on track, something that is taking more effort, etc.)

2. What is your <u>commitment</u> in this area? What would it look like if it were going exactly the way you want it to go?

3. Think of a time when things in this area were going very well. What adjectives would you use to describe yourself at that time? (e.g. excited, energized, motivated…)

4. What is keeping you from being that way now? What, or who, do you have a complaint about?

5. What adjectives would you use to describe yourself now while things are not going well in that area? (e.g. frustrated, powerless, angry…)

6. What unmet <u>expectations</u> do you have that have caused you to be this way?

7. If these expectations were met, could you be the way you were as described in the answer to question 3? Yes / No?

8. What actions are you willing to commit to taking to influence your expectations to be met, or to give up your complaint about them and be powerful in the face of adversity?

Transformation Blueprint

I have found the following questions and thought processes helpful in planning transformation. Keep in mind that if your idea is truly transformative, you will not be clear on the exact answers to these questions, and your responses may change as you progress through your journey and you gain more clarity. But the most important step is to get started and this process gives you a place to start. Some comments have been provided in *italics* to guide you through the process.

1. In what area are you committed to creating a transformation? (Pick one; be specific)
   This could be a specific result that you are responsible for, or a certain aspect of the culture.

2. What bold future are you declaring? What will it look like when you are there?
   A. Quantitative Results: *There needs to be a tangible way to measure these and know whether the result was achieved or not.*

   B. Qualitative Results: *These are sometimes more subject to interpretation, like certain aspects of the culture. But, the contrast between the before and after state should be observable.*

3. What key milestones must you reach along the way to achieve this transformation? (Put a target date next to each).
   If you are truly working on a transformation (vs. change), you will not know all the milestones and you will need to be flexible in adjusting these as you go, in order to stay true to your commitment. At this stage, use your best judgment based on what you know, capture the key milestones that you must work toward, and put dates next to them so that you can check your progress along the way and make adjustments.

4. Who are the key people you are committed to energizing and involving in making your vision a reality?
   Although your transformation may ultimately involve a large number of people, it is important that you identify a few people whom you will be intentional about energizing. I would put 2 to 5 people on the initial list. You can always expand the list later.

5. What is the greatest barrier to progress?
   By now, you know that you are the greatest barrier to progress because you have either created, contributed to, or have tolerated the existing barriers in place, but this question is geared toward the external barriers that must be addressed.

6. What persistent complaint have you had about this barrier? Are you willing to give it up and get in action?

You need to be straight with yourself about this. It is always helpful to just sit and write down all the complaints you have about the situation on a piece of paper. Your persistent complaint will jump out at you. The key is to assess whether your attitude and behavior toward that problem are helping or hurting your ability to solve the problem. If it is the latter, then all there is to do is to give up the complaint.

7. **What step(s) are you committed to taking immediately in the direction of removing/neutralizing this barrier? By when will you complete these?**
   Specific and immediate actions and dates are necessary for any of the above to do any good. Without this, the rest of the work you have done so far won't matter. You can start small if you want, to get some wins under your belt. You don't have to have a great start, you just need to have a start!

8. **What language or behaviors need to be altered in your organization to shift the culture to being "on the court" versus being "in the stands?"**
   You can start with your wish-list, but narrow it down to 1 to 2 critical aspects of the culture, such as language or behaviors.

9. **Are you committed to role-modeling this shift? How?**
   Culture transformation must start with you. Make a commitment to model specific behavior and language, and go to work on

yourself. I would strongly urge you to declare your commitments to others around you and ask them to help you stay on track. This helps you remain in action and it also sends a strong signal to others that you are serious about leading a culture transformation.

10. What are key opportunities for you to increase your competence? What steps will you take to accomplish this and by when?

NOTES

Concepts I have learned:

Things I discovered about myself and my tendencies that I didn't see previously:

Actions I am committed to taking and the date by which I will complete them:

ABOUT THE AUTHOR

Amir Ghannad is a leadership coach, a sought after keynote speaker in the US and abroad, and the founder of The Ghannad Group LLC, which offers coaching and consulting services in the area of leadership effectiveness and culture transformation.

For the past 30 years, Amir has held leadership positions in the US, Southeast Asia, and Europe at Procter and Gamble, Sunny Delight Beverages, and Campbell Soup Company. Amir has effectively led multi-national and multi-functional teams in delivering superior results through his ability to rally teams around a common vision.

A registered corporate coach and an accomplished trainer of courses such as Seven Habits of Highly Effective People, The Speed of Trust, The Mind Gym, and many others, Amir has designed and delivered numerous customized learning events that have helped organizations successfully achieve results in a variety of business situations.

Amir is proficient in using an array of tools and methodologies to facilitate teams through the process of strategy development and deployment, organizational assessment and design, high performance organization development, transition management, and leadership development.

Amir holds B.S. and M.S. degrees in Mechanical Engineering from the Georgia Institute of Technology and a MBA from Wilmington University. Amir and his wife, Connie, live in Atlanta, Georgia, have been married for 33 years, and have a son and a daughter.

CONNECT WITH AMIR

I would love to hear about your challenges and your triumphs.

Contact Amir at
ttl@theghannadgroup.com

For more about Amir, The Ghannad Group, and to read his blog, visit:
www.theghannadgroup.com

Subscribe to The Transformative Leader Podcast
theghannadgroup.com/podcast

Find Amir on Social Media:
Twitter @amirghannad
Instagram @theghannadgroup
Linkedin linkedin.com/in/aaghannad